Giant Book
of DIRTY
JOKES

Compiled by
"Mr. J"

CASTLE BOOKS

This edition published by
CASTLE BOOKS ®
A division of BOOK SALES, INC.
276 Fifth Avenue Suite 206
New York, New York 10001
USA

Printed by special permission of Citadel Press (a division of Lyle Stuart, Inc.)

The Giant Book of Dirty Jokes was originally published in three volumes:
The World's Best Dirty Jokes, copyright © 1976 by Lyle Stuart, Inc.
More of the World's Best Dirty Jokes, copyright © 1979 by Citadel Press
(a division of Lyle Stuart, Inc.)
Still More of the World's Best Dirty Jokes, copyright © 1981 by Citadel Press
(a division of Lyle Stuart, Inc.)

ISBN-13: 978-0-89009-812-7

Printed in the United States of America

TABLE OF CONTENTS

Mr. "J"

THE

World's
Best
Dirty
Jokes

Drawings by Arthur Robins

May all your pleasures be long ones
—and may all your days be filled with love.

Acknowledgments

"Mr. J.," who compiled this book, is grateful to a number of people who helped to judge the jokes that follow:

    Morris Cargill (of Jamaica, W.I.)
    William M. Gaines
    Al Goldstein
    Carlos Gonzalez
    John Hearne (of Jamaica, W.I.)
    Liz Hearne (of Jamaica, W.I.)
    Carole Livingston
    David Ross
    Morris Sorkin
    Rory John Stuart
    Sandra Lee Stuart
    Allan J. Wilson

—and to Dick Manning, Paul Schumer, and the late Frank Edwards, who told us many of them in their masterful manner. . . .

One morning recently
A young woman
Got out of bed
Slipped into her robe
Raised the shade
Uncovered the parrot
Put on the coffee pot
Answered the phone
And heard a masculine voice say:
"Hello, honey. My ship just hit port
And I'm coming right over."
So the young lady
Took the coffee pot off the stove
Covered up the parrot
Pulled down the shade
Took off her robe
Got into bed
and heard the parrot mumble,
"Kee-rist, what a short day that was!"

Reggie owned an elephant, but the cost of feeding it was getting out of hand. Then he got an idea. He had seen elephants lift one leg, and even two legs. Once in a circus he'd even seen an elephant lift three legs in the air and stand on just one.

So Reggie announced to the world that he'd pay ten thousand dollars to anyone who could make his elephant stand in the air on no legs. However, each person who wanted to try would have to pay a hundred dollars.

People came from near and far. They tried everything from coaxing to hypnotism, but no one could make the elephant rise up in the air.

Then one day a blue convertible drove up and a little man got out and addressed Reggie: "Is it true that you'll pay ten thousand dollars if I make your elephant get off all four legs?"

"Yes," Reggie said, "but you've got to pay one hundred dollars to try."

The little man handed Reggie a hundred-dollar bill. Then he went back to the car and took out a metal club. He walked up to the elephant and looked him in the eye. Then he walked behind the elephant and swung hard, hitting the elephant smack on the balls. The elephant let out a roar and flew up into the air.

After the little man had collected his ten thousand dollars, Reggie was very depressed. He'd only taken in eight thousand dollars and now he'd not only lost a couple of grand but still had the problem of feeding and housing the elephant.

Suddenly Reggie got another inspiration. He knew that elephants could move their heads up and down, but he had never seen one move from side to side. So he announced that he would pay ten thousand dollars to anyone who could make his elephant move his head from side to side. However, each person who wanted to try would have to pay one hundred dollars.

People came from near and far. They paid their hundred and they tried, but, of course, none succeeded.

Then just when things were going well, a familiar blue convertible drove up and the little man came out. He addressed Reggie: "Is it true that you'll pay me ten thousand dollars if I can make your elephant move his head from side to side?"

"Yes," said Reggie, "but you've got to pay a hundred dollars to try."

The little man handed Reggie the hundred dollars. Then he returned to his car and took out his metal club. He walked up to the elephant.

"Do you remember me?" he asked.

The elephant nodded by shaking his head up and down.

"Do you want me to do it again?"

The elephant quickly shook his head . . . no.

This man was in bed with a married woman when they heard the door open. "Oh my God," she gasped, "it's my husband! Quick, hide in the closet!"

The man hurried into the closet and closed the door. Suddenly, he heard a small voice saying, "It's very dark in here."

"Who is that?" he asked.

"That's my mother out there," the small voice said. "And now I'm going to scream."

"Please don't!" the man said.

"Okay, but it'll cost you money," the boy said. "Here's five dollars."

"I'm going to scream!" said the small voice.

"Okay, here's ten dollars!"

"I'm going to scream," the small voice said.

"Here's twenty dollars."

Finally, when the boy turned down thirty-five dollars, the man said, "All I have is forty dollars."

"I'll take it!"

At last, the husband left and the man was able to get out of the closet and make a hasty exit.

That afternoon, the mother took the boy with her on a shopping trip.

"I want to get that bicycle," he said.

The mother said, "No, you can't. It costs too much money."

The boy said, "I've got forty dollars."

The mother said, "Where would you get forty dollars?"

The boy wouldn't talk. She began to berate him. He refused to respond. She slapped his face. He stood stoicly. Finally, twisting his arm, she dragged him into the nearby neighborhood church and approached the parish priest. "Father, my son has forty dollars and he won't tell me where he got it. Maybe you can find out?"

The priest nodded. He led the boy into a confessional booth. The boy sat on one side and the priest in the other. The boy said, "It's very dark in here...."

And the priest said, "Now, don't you start that again!"

Then there is the story of the eighty-year-old Italian roué who called on his doctor.

"Professore, I would like you to examine me. To see if I am sexually fit."

"Very well, let me see your sex organs, please."

The aged patient replied, "Eccoli," and stuck out his index finger and his tongue.

A man who was frightened of dentists delayed seeing one until he only had six teeth left in his mouth.

The dentist examined him and said: "These teeth are finished. Let me pull them out. Let me do root canal work and all those other things I do, and you'll have a complete new set of choppers in your mouth. Beautiful you'll look, and chewing problems you'll no longer have."

The man was dubious. "I'm a physical coward, Doc. I can't stand pain."

"Who said anything about pain? I'm a painless dentist!"

"You say it, but how do I know if it's true?"

"Not to worry," the dentist said. "I did a job exactly like this for another man. I'll give you his name and you can phone him right now. Ask if I caused him any pain."

So the man telephoned George Kaplan in Brooklyn.

"Mr. Kaplan," he said, "my name is Al Goldstein. You don't know me, but I'm in the office of your dentist and he says he did a big job on your teeth. Is that correct?"

"Correct it is," Kaplan agreed.

"Okay," said Goldstein. "Now I want you to tell me the honest truth. Did it hurt? Tell me, yes or no?"

"A yes or no I can't give you," said Kaplan, "but I can give you a fr'instance. Every Sunday I go rowing in Prospect Park..."

"So?" said Goldstein.

"So," said Kaplan, "our dentist finished with me in December. Now it's June and it's Sunday, and, as usual, I'm in my rowboat on the Prospect Park lake. Suddenly, one of the oars slip away. When I reach over to grab it, my balls get caught in the oarlock. Would you believe it, Mr. Goldstein, it was the first time in six months that my teeth didn't hurt!"

An elephant was having an awful time in the jungle because a horsefly kept biting her near her tail and there was nothing she could do about it. She kept swinging her trunk, but he was far out of reach.

A little sparrow observed this and suddenly flew down and snipped the horsefly in half with his beak.

"Oh, thank you!" said the elephant. "That was such a relief."

"My pleasure, ma'am," said the sparrow.

"Listen, Mr. Sparrow, if there's anything I can ever do for you, don't hesitate to ask."

The sparrow hesitated. "Well, ma'am —" he said.

"What is it," said the elephant. "You needn't be shy with me."

"Well," said the sparrow, "the truth is that all my life I wondered how it would feel to fuck an elephant."

"Go right ahead," said the elephant. "Be my guest!"

The sparrow flew around behind the elephant and began to fuck away. Up above them, a monkey in the tree watched and began to get very excited. He started to masturbate. This shook a coconut loose and it fell from the tree, hitting the elephant smack on the head.

"Ouch!" said the elephant.

At which point, the sparrow looked over from behind and said, "Am I hurting you, dear?"

The late Dr. Kinsey was questioning a group of men about the number of times they had sex relations with members of the opposite sex.

In response to his question, a group of men raised their hands to indicate that they had sex every night. Then some said they had relations ten times a month. A small group said they only did it about four times a month.

Finally, every man in the room had been accounted for except one man who was sitting in the corner.

Dr. Kinsey moved closer to him. "All right. How many of you have sex relations only once a year?"

"Me! Me!" the man piped up, waving his hand wildly and wearing an ear-to-ear smile.

"Fine," said Dr. Kinsey. "But why are you so happy about it?"

"Because tonight's the night!" the man explained with glee. "Tonight's the night!"

So this old man went into Ma Agnew's whorehouse and said, "Listen, Ma, I want a girl with gonorrhea."

The madam nodded and sent him upstairs to a room. Then she called one of her favorites for him. The girl came into the room and started to undress when he asked, "Do you have gonorrhea?"

"Gonorrhea? I should say not!" she said.

The old man sent her back. The madam summoned another girl and said, "Shirley, you go upstairs and tell this old codger that you have the clap. Okay? Let's do what we have to to make him happy."

The girl agreed and went upstairs, and when the old man asked, "Do you have gonorrhea?" she smiled and said, "Of course I do!"

"Good!" he said. "Let's get it on."

They got into bed together and fucked for about ten minutes. When it was over and they lay side by side, the girl named Shirley said, "Listen, grandpa, I've got a confession to make. I don't really have gonorrhea."

The old man smiled. "Now you do," he said.

He went to his doctor full of anger. "Doc," he said, "I feel like killing my wife. You've got to help me. You've got to tell me what to do."

The doctor decided on how to best handle the case. "Look," he said, "here are some pills. You take these twice a day and they'll enable you to fuck your wife six times a day. If you do this for thirty days, you'll fuck her to death."

"Wonderful, doc," said the grateful patient. "I think I'll take her to Miami Beach so there won't be anything to interfere with us and no one will be suspicious."

He left with a bottle of pills in his hand and a smile on his face.

Nearly a month passed. The doctor flew to Miami Beach for a medical convention. There, on Lincoln Road, he saw his patient coming along in a wheelchair, just managing to move forward.

"What happened?" the doctor asked. "What happened?"

"Don't worry, doc," the patient reassured him, "two more days and she'll be dead."

An old man made it shakily through the door to Joe Conforte's Mustang Ranch, outside Reno, Nevada.

The receptionist stared at him. "You gotta be in the wrong place," she exclaimed. "What are you looking for?"

"Ain't this the famous Mustang? Ain't this where you allus got forty-five girls ready 'n' able?"

The receptionist looked perplexed. "Ready for what?"

"I want a girl," the old man rasped. "I wanna get laid."

"How old are you, Pop?" she asked.

"Ninety-two," he replied.

"Ninety-two? Pop, you've *had* it!"

"Oh," said the old man, a little disconcerted as his trembling fingers reached for his wallet. "How much do I owe you?"

The scene was Elaine's Restaurant on Second Avenue in Manhattan on a crowded Saturday night. A stranger walked in from the street and pompously announced that, even with a blindfold on, he could identify any wine.

The challenge was immediately accepted. A dark cloth was placed over his eyes and wine after wine was handed to him.

"Lafite-Rothschild, 1958," he would announce. Or, "Bernkasteler Badstube, 1951." And he was always right.

Finally, someone handed him a glass he couldn't identify. He sipped, and then he sipped again. Suddenly he spat it out and pulled off the blindfold.

"Hell, man! This is urine! Plain fresh urine!"

"Yes," said a small voice in the background, "but *whose*?"

This gay chap was looking in a sex shop window. He saw a large rubber cock that appealed to him, and he ventured inside.

When the clerk came to wait on him, he pointed to the big black penis in the window. "I'll take that one," he said.

"Should I wrap it or just put it in a bag?" asked the clerk.

"Neither," said the customer. "I'll just eat it right here."

Jim and Joe were two friends who shared an apartment together in Chicago. One day, Jim came home to find Joe weeping into his hands. "I'm so unlucky! So unlucky!" he moaned.

"You're always saying that, and it isn't so," Jim said.

"It is! It is!" Joe said. "I'm the most unlucky fellow you know!"

"What happened now?"

"Well, I met this beautiful woman on Madison Street. We got to talking and we stopped off at a small bar and had a few drinks. Wow! We got really mellow. When she suggested that I go to her place, I thought my luck had changed."

"It sounds like it did," Jim said.

"Minutes after we entered her apartment I was in bed with her. I was just starting to climax when we heard the door bang open."

"It's my husband!" she said.

"I didn't even have time to grab a towel. I bounded for the window and just managed to climb out, hanging on the ledge by my hands, when he barged in.

"He sized up the scene immediately, and then he saw my hands hanging on for dear life. He came to the window and started pounding my knuckles with a hammer. Then he took out his cock and pissed all over me. Then he slammed the window on my bloody fingers.

21

Then, as if I didn't have trouble enough, two old ladies on the street saw me hanging there stark naked, and they started screaming for the police. The cops came and I was arrested. Now do you see what I mean when I say I'm unlucky?"

"Nonsense," Jim said. "You're upset, but an experience like that could happen to anyone."

"You don't understand," Joe said, "When the cops came to arrest me, I looked down and my feet were only four inches from the ground. Now do you see what I mean when I say I'm unlucky?"

Jones took his nymphomaniac wife to the doctor for treatment. "This is one hot potato of a lady, doctor," he said. "Maybe you can do something for her? She goes for any man, and I get very jealous."

"We'll see," the doctor said. He directed Mrs. Jones into his examining room, closed the door behind him and told her to undress. Then he told her to get up onto the examining table on her stomach.

The moment he touched her buttocks, she began to moan and squirm. It was too much for him to resist, and he climbed up on top of her and began to screw her.

Jones suddenly heard moans and groans coming from the examination room. Unable to control himself, he pushed open the door, to be confronted by the sight of the doctor astride his wife and banging away.

"Doctor, what are you doing?" he asked.

The flustered doctor said, "Oh, it's you, Jones? I'm only taking your wife's temperature!"

Jones opened his switchblade knife and began to hone it on his sleeve very deliberately. "Doc," he said, "when you take that thing out, it better have numbers on it!"

A midget went into a whorehouse. None of the girls really wanted to serve him, so finally they drew lots and Mitzi was unlucky and went up to the room with him.

A minute later, there was a loud scream. The Madam and all of the girls charged up the staircase and into the room. Mitzi lay on the floor in a dead faint. Standing next to the bed was the midget, nude, and with a three foot cock hanging down and almost touching the floor.

The girls were dumbfounded by the sight. Finally, one of them regained her composure to say, "Sir, would you mind if we felt it? We've never seen anything like that before."

The midget sighed. "Okay, honey. But only touching. No sucking. I used to be six feet tall."

A ventriloquist was driving in the country when he was attracted to a large farm. He asked for and was given a tour.

As he was shown through the barn, the ventriloquist thought he'd have some fun. He proceeded to make one of the horses talk.

The hired hand, wide-eyed with fear, rushed from the barn to the farmer. "Sam," he shouted, "those animals are talking! If that little sheep says anything about me, it's a damned lie!"

The salesman stopped at a farmhouse one evening to ask for room and board for the night. The farmer told him there was no vacant room.

"I could let you sleep with my daughter," the farmer said, "if you promise not to bother her."

The salesman agreed.

After a hearty supper, he was led to the room. He undressed in the dark, slipped into bed, and felt the farmer's daughter at his side.

The next morning he asked for his bill.

"It'll be just two dollars, since you had to share the bed," the farmer said.

"Your daughter was very cold," the salesman said.

"Yes, I know," said the farmer. "We're going to bury her today."

Charlie was visiting an old friend and his wife for dinner. When the time came to leave, his car wouldn't start, and it was too late to call the local service station.

The husband urged Charlie to stay over. There was no spare bed in the house; there wasn't even a sofa. So Charlie would have to sleep with the husband and wife.

No sooner had the husband fallen asleep when the wife tapped Charlie on the shoulder and motioned for him to come over to her.

"I couldn't do that," he whispered. "Your husband is my best friend!"

"Listen, sugar," she whispered back, "there ain't nothing in the whole wide world could wake him up now."

"I can't believe that," Charlie said. "Certainly if I get on top of you and screw you, he'll wake up, won't he?"

"Sugar, he certainly won't. If you don't believe me, pluck a hair out of his asshole and see if that wakes him."

Charlie did just that. He was amazed when the husband remained asleep. So he climbed over to the wife's side of the bed and fucked her. When he finished, he climbed back to his own side. It wasn't long before she tapped him on the shoulder and beckoned him over again. Again he pulled a hair to determine if his old friend was asleep. This went on eight times during the night. Each time Charlie screwed the woman, he first pulled out one of the husband's asshole hairs.

The ninth time he pulled a hair, the husband awoke and muttered: "Listen, Charlie, old pal, I don't mind you fucking my wife, but for Pete's sake, stop using my ass for a scoreboard!"

Muldoon had died from dysentery. When they went to prepare him for burial, he was still excreting. The undertaker thought about it for a moment, then went out and returned with a large cork. He corked up Muldoon's ass.

A couple of hours later, O'Shawnessy and Ryan came to carry the body down to the living room for the wake.

Ryan led the way as they started walking down the stairs slowly. Soft organ music was playing in the background and all the guests stood about with their heads bowed.

Suddenly, the cork came out and excretion came pouring down on top of Ryan's head. He promptly dropped the body and Culdoon's corpse came hurtling down the stairs.

The undertaker rushed up to Ryan. "What the hell did you do, man?"

And Ryan said calmly, "Listen, man, if that bastard can shit, he can walk!"

When the delegate from the emerging African nation was in Moscow, he watched a game of Russian roulette. Someone put the barrel of a pistol to his head and pulled the trigger. One of the six chambers contained a real bullet.

Now the Russian delegate was visiting the African nation.

"We would like to show you our version of roulette," the Ambassador said. "We call this African roulette."

"How do you play it?"

The Ambassador pointed to six buxom African girls sitting in a circle. "Any of these girls will give you a blow job."

"Where is the roulette part? Where is the jeopardy?" the Russian asked.

"Well," said the African Ambassador, "one of the girls is a cannibal."

L ittle Willie had a gambling problem. He'd bet on anything. One day, Willie's father consulted his teacher.

The teacher said, "Mr. Gaines, I think I know how to teach Willie a real lesson. We'll trap him into a big wager that he'll lose."

Willie's father agreed to cooperate with the plan.

The next day at school, the teacher watched Willie making wagers with the other children, and she said, "Willie, I want you to remain after class."

When the others had left the classroom, Willie walked up to the teacher. Before she could open her mouth, he said, "Don't say it, Miss B.; I know what you're going to say, but you're a liar!"

"Willie!" the startled teacher said. "What are you talking about?"

"You're a fake!" Willie continued. "How can I believe anything you tell me? You've got this blond hair on top, but I ve seen your bush and it's pitch black!"

Trying to keep her cool, the teacher said, "Willie, that isn't true."

"I'll bet a dollar it is!" Willie challenged.

The teacher saw her chance to teach Willie his lesson. "Make it five dollars and you have a bet," she said.

"You're on!" Willie whipped out a five-dollar bill.

Before anyone could come into the room, Miss B.

dropped her panties, spread her legs, and showed Willie that her pubic hair was as blond as the hair on top of her head.

Willie hung his head. "You win,' he said, handing her the fiver.

Miss B. couldn't wait for him to leave so she could get to a phone to call his father. She reported what had happened. "Mr. Gaines," she said, "I think we've finally taught him his lesson."

"The hell we have,' the father muttered. "This morning Willie bet me ten dollars that he'd see your cunt before the day was over."

The famous Greek ship owner, Ori Oristotle, was having a house built on a large piece of land in Greece. He said to the architect, "Don't disturb that tree over there because directly under that tree is where I had my first sex.

"How sentimental, Mr. Oristotle," the architect said. "Right under that tree."

"Yes," continued Ori Oristotle, "And don't touch that tree over there either. Because that's where her mother stood watching while I was having my first sex."

"Her mother just stood there while you were fucking her daughter?" the architect asked.

"Yes," said the Greek ship owner.

"But, Mr. Oristotle, what did her mother say?"

"Baaaa."

rs. Keller had a very talented parrot. At her dinner parties he was the center of attention, for she had trained him to repeat what the butler said when he announced the guests as they arrived.

The parrot had only one failing: He loved to fuck chickens. Every chance he got, he would fly over the fence into the yard of the farmer next door and fuck his chickens.

The farmer complained to Mrs. Keller, and finally she laid the law down to the parrot.

"Bertram," she said, "you better listen to me! The next time you go into Farmer Whalen's yard and fuck another chicken I'm going to punish you plenty!"

The parrot hung his head to show he understood. But two days later, he couldn't resist temptation and over the fence he went. He was deep into screwing his third hen when Farmer Whalen spotted him and chased him. Whalen complained again to Mrs. Keller.

"Now you're going to get it!" she said. She got a pair of barber's shears and clipped all the feathers from the top of the parrot's head.

That night, Mrs. Keller threw one of her gala parties. She put the parrot on top of the piano.

"Bertram," she said, "you've been a rotten old thing. Tonight you're to sit here all night. No wandering around and no playing the way you usually do!"

And so, feeling rather disconsolate, the parrot sat on the piano. As the butler announced the guests, Bertram performed as usual, repeating the names. The butler said, "Mr. Arnold Levy and Lady Stella," and the parrot said, "Mr. Arnold Levy and Lady Stella." The butler said, "Mr. and Mrs. Robert Salomon," and the parrot said, "Mr. and Mrs. Robert Salomon."

Then two bald-headed men entered the room. Without waiting for the butler to announce them, the parrot shouted: "All right, you chicken-fuckers! Up here on the piano with me!"

A farmer sent his fifteen-year-old son to town and, as a birthday present, handed him a duck. "See if you can get a girl in exchange for this," he said.

The lad met a prostitute and said, "It's my birthday and all I've got is this duck? Would you be willing to —?"

"Sure," she said. "I'm sentimental about birthdays. And besides, I've never owned a duck."

Afterwards, she said, "Do you know, for a fifteen-year-old, you're quite a lay. If you do it again, I'll give you back your duck. '

"Sure," said the boy.

When his pleasurable work was through, he started on his way home. While he was crossing the main street in the village, the duck suddenly flew out of his hands and was hit by a passing beer truck. The driver of the truck felt sorry for the boy and gave him $2.

When he got home, his father asked, "How did you make out?"

The son said: "I got a fuck a duck, a duck for a fuck, and two dollars for a fucked-up duck."

Lee and Larry were a pair of winos. They woke up with the shakes one afternoon to find they had only forty cents between them. Lee began to climb the walls, but Larry said calmly, "Look, old man, give me the forty cents and I'll show you how we can drink free all day." So they went into a delicatessen, and Lee bought a frankfurter, which he stuck in Larry's fly.

Next, they went into a nearby bar and ordered drinks. When the bartender asked for his money, Lee got down on the floor and started sucking the frankfurter. The bartender screamed, "You fucking queers, get out of here!"

They repeated the scene in bar after bar until they had toured a dozen of them. Finally, Lee complained, "Listen, Larry, it was a great scheme but my knees are getting sore from hitting the floor so much."

Larry shook his head. "You should complain," he said. "We lost the hot dog after the second bar!"

Inflation was getting out of hand so Joe suggested to his wife, Louise, that they try a unique way to save some money on the side.

"Every time I lay you, I'll give you a dollar for your piggy bank," he said.

A few weeks later, they decided to open the piggy bank. Out tumbled a bunch of dollars, but these were mixed with a rich cluster of fives, tens and twenties.

"Louise," asked Joe, "where did you get all that money? Each time we fucked I only gave you a dollar.'

"So?" she said. "Do you think everyone is as stingy as you?"

The agent for a beautiful actress discovered one day that she had been selling her body at a hundred dollars a night.

The agent, who had long lusted for her, hadn't dreamed that she had been so easily obtainable. He approached her, told her how much she turned him on and how much he wanted to make it with her.

She agreed to spend the night with him, but said he would have to pay her the same hundred dollars that the other customers did.

He scratched his head, considered it, and then asked, "Don't I even get my agent's ten percent as a deduction?"

"No siree," she said. "If you want it, you're going to have to pay full price for it, just like the other Johns."

The agent didn't like that at all, but he agreed.

That night, she came to his apartment after her performance at a local night club. The agent screwed her at midnight, after turning out all the lights.

At 1 A.M., she was awakened again. Again she was vigorously screwed. In a little while, she was awakened again, and again she was screwed. The actress was impressed with her lover's vitality.

"My God," she whispered in the dark, "you are

virile. I never realized how lucky I was to have you for my agent."

"I'm not your agent, lady," a strange voice answered. "He's at the door taking tickets!"

A drunk walked into a bar crying. One of the other men at the bar asked him what happened.

"I did a horrible thing," sniffled the drunk. "Just a few hours ago I sold my wife to someone for a bottle of scotch."

"That *is* awful," said the other guy. "And now she's gone and you want her back, right?"

"Right," said the drunk, still crying.

"You're sorry you sold her because you realized too late that you love her, right?"

"Oh, no," said the drunk. "I want her back because I'm thirsty again!"

The butcher lived in an apartment over his shop. One night he was awakened by strange noises coming from below. He tiptoed downstairs and observed that his 19-year-old daughter was sitting on the chopping block and masturbating with a liverwurst. He sighed and tiptoed back to bed.

The next morning, one of his customers came in and asked for some liverwurst. The butcher explained that he didn't have any.

The lady was annoyed. She pointed and said, "No liverwurst, eh? Well, what's that hanging on the hook right over there?"

The butcher frowned at her and replied, "That, lady, is my son-in-law."

The couple visited a sex clinic to complain that their sex life had become a bore.

Each night the man would arrive home. His wife would prepare supper. After supper, they'd watch two hours of TV. Immediately after the eleven o'clock news, they would get into bed. From that point on, every move was routine.

"No wonder," the sex consultant said. "You've made sex monotonous. Stop living on a schedule. Get into sex when you feel like it. Don't wait until eleven o'clock each night. Do it when you get into the mood."

The couple agreed to try the advice. They returned the following week.

"How did things work out?" the sex doctor asked.

The man and his wife were beaming. "It worked! It worked!"

"Tell me about it," said the doctor.

"Well, two nights after we saw you, we were eating supper when I noticed that although it was only eight-thirty, I had this great erection. Sweetie pie here was staring at it with longing eyes. So I didn't wait for any shower or any news broadcast. Instead, I reached out, ripped off her blouse and her bra. Then I pulled off her panties. I flung her to the floor right under the table. Then I unzipped my fly and pulled out my cock and we began to fuck. Man, we fucked like we have never fucked before."

"That's wonderful!" said the sex expert. "I told you it would work if you did it when the spirit moved!"

"Only one thing," the man said a little sadly. "They're not going to let us come back to Howard Johnson's restaurant any more."

A mother and her daughter came to the doctor's office. The mother asked the doctor to examine her daughter.

"She has been having some strange symptoms and I'm worried about her," the mother said.

The doctor examined the daughter carefully. Then he announced, "Madam, I believe your daughter is pregnant."

The mother gasped. "That's nonsense!" she said. "Why, my little girl has nothing whatsoever to do with men." She turned to the girl. "You don't, do you, dear?"

"No, Mumsy," said the girl. "Why, you know that I have never so much as kissed a man!"

The doctor looked from mother to daughter, and back again. Then, silently he stood up and walked to the window. He stared out. He continued staring until the mother felt compelled to ask, "Doctor, is there something wrong out there?"

"No, Madam," said the doctor. "It's just that the last time anything like this happened, a star appeared in the East and I was looking to see if another one was going to show up. '

The state senator was seeking votes for his election campaign for Congress and decided to visit the local Indian reservation. He stood in the large community hall and told the Indians what he would do for them if he was elected.

"I think the time has come when you people deserve to really control your own destiny," he said.

From the crowded auditorium came a responding chorus, "Um gwalla gwalla!"

The senator smiled. "Furthermore," he continued, "I think the time has come for your old people to get really good pensions."

Again came a chorus of "Um gwalla gwalla!"

He nodded approvingly. "One more thing," he said, "if I m elected, I'm not going to rest until every one of you Indians gets full citizenship with all the rights every full-blooded American has."

Once again, there was a loud responding roar of "Um gwalla gwalla!"

After his speech, the senator was given a guided tour of the reservation. He saw a high fence and asked what it contained.

The guide said: "That the place where we kept bulls. Now just empty grazing ground. No bulls now."

"Good!" he said, and started to climb over the fence.

His guide warned: "Be careful, senator! You go in there you liable to step in much um gwalla gwalla."

The parish priest couldn't resist the pretty young girl. She was reciting her confession, and it was all too much for him. He told her to come with him to his room. There, he placed his arm around her.

"Did the young man do this to you?" he asked.

"Yes, Father, and worse," the girl replied.

"Hmm," said the priest. He kissed her.

"Did he do this?"

"Yes, Father, and worse," the girl said.

"Did he do this?" the priest asked, and he lifted her skirt and fingered her bush.

"Yes, Father, and worse."

By this time, the priest was thoroughly aroused. He pulled the girl down onto the rug and inserted his penis, breathing heavily as he asked, "Did he manage to do this?"

"Yes, Father, and worse," said the girl.

When the priest had finished with the girl, he asked, "He did this too, and worse? My dear daughter, what worse could he have done?"

"Well," the shy young girl said, "I think, Father, that he's given me gonorrhea."

Little Red Riding Hood was walking through the woods on her way to visit her grandmother, when suddenly a wolf jumped out from behind a tree.

"Ah-ha!" the wolf said, "Now I've got you. And I'm going to eat you!"

"Eat! Eat! Eat!" Little Red Riding Hood said angrily. "Damn it! Doesn't anybody fuck anymore?"

The Frenchman and the Italian were in the woods hunting together when suddenly a voluptuous blonde girl raced across their path, totally nude.

"Would I love to eat that? *Oui, oui!*" the Frenchman said, smacking his lips.

So the Italian shot her.

He had heard that a certain whorehouse in Great Neck, New York, had an unusual reputation for the bizarre. So he drove to the place and, once inside, asked the Madam if she had anything unusual for him to try.

"Things are pretty slow today," she said, "but I do have one number you might enjoy." She went on to describe a New Jersey hen that had been trained to do blow jobs.

"We've got her here, but only for the day."

The visitor could hardly believe it, but he paid the fee and went into a room with the hen. After a frustrating hour of trying to force his cock into the hen's mouth, he figured out that he was dealing with nothing but a plain old chicken. He left.

Thinking about it later, he decided that he had had so much fun trying that he returned the next day and asked the Madam, "Do you have anything new today?"

"Come this way," she said, and led him to a dark room where a group of men were looking through a one-way mirror. He saw that they were watching a girl trying to make it with a dog.

"Wow!" he said to the man standing next to him. "This is really great!"

The man replied, "Man, it ain't nothin'! You shoulda been here yesterday and seen the guy with the chicken."

The recruit had just arrived at a Foreign Legion post in the desert. He asked his corporal what the men did for recreation.

The corporal smiled wisely and said, "You'll see."

The young man was puzzled. "Well, you've got more than a hundred men on this base and I don't see a single woman."

"You'll see," the corporal repeated.

That afternoon, three hundred camels were herded in the corral. At a signal, the men seemed to go wild. They leaped into the corral and began to screw the camels.

The recruit saw the corporal hurrying past him and grabbed his arm. "I see what you mean, but I don't understand," he said. "There must be three hundred of those camels and only about a hundred of us. Why is everybody rushing? Can't a man take his time?"

"What?" exclaimed the corporal, startled. "And get stuck with an ugly one?"

She was wearing a very tight skirt, and when she tried to board the Fifth Avenue bus she found she couldn't lift her leg. She reached back and unzipped her zipper. It didn't seem to do any good, so she reached back and unzipped it again.

Suddenly the man behind her lifted her up and put her on the top step.

"How dare you?" she demanded.

"Well, lady," he said, "by the time you unzipped my fly for the second time I thought we were good friends."

This Chinese laundryman complained to the doctor that he was very constipated. The doctor gave him a prescription for a good physic. "Come to my office in a few days," said the doctor, "and let me know how it works '

A few days later, the Chinaman visited the doctor.

"Have you moved yet?' asked the doctor.

"No, sir, me no moovee, me no moovee."

The doctor scratched his head and then gave the man a prescription for twice as much. Three days later, when the man reported to the doctor again, he said that he still hadn't moved and the doctor gave him a triple dose, and he said, "Come back to see me in two days and let me know just what is happening."

Two days later, the man came back.

"Well," said the doctor, "have you moved yet?"

"No, sir, me no moovee yet. Me moovee tomorrow, though. House full of shit."

This fellow rushed into a crowded tavern on Saturday night. Men and women stood three-deep at the bar. Our man, who felt nature calling strongly, looked about him but couldn't see anything that resembled a john.

He saw a stairway and bounded up the steps to the second floor in his increasingly desperate search. Just as his bowels threatened to erupt, he spotted a one-foot by one-foot hole in the floor. Now, at the end of his control, he decided to take advantage of the hole. He dropped his pants, hunched over it, and did his thing.

Thoroughly relieved and relaxed, he sauntered down the steps to find, to his surprise, that the bar which had been so crowded a few minutes ago, was now empty.

"Hey!" he yelled to the seemingly empty room, "Where is everyone?"

From behind the bar a voice responded, "Where were you when the shit hit the fan?"

Aman went to have plastic surgery on his penis. The surgeon examined him and asked, "What happened?'

"Well, doc, I live in a trailer camp," the man explained, "And from where I am I can see this lovely chick next door. She's blonde and she's built like a brick shithouse. She's so horny that every night I see her take a hot dog from the refrigerator and stick it in a hole in the floor of her trailer. Then she gets down and masturbates herself on the hot dog."

"And?" prompted the doctor.

"Well," said the man, "I felt this was a lot of wasted pussy, so one day I got under the trailer and when she put the hot dog in the hole, I removed it and substituted my dick.

"It was a great idea and everything was going real good, too. Then someone knocked at her door, and she jumped off my hot dog and tried to kick it under the stove."

A population control program had been introduced to the island, but the medical men were having trouble getting the women to take their birth control pills. They decided, therefore, to concentrate on teaching the men to wear condoms.

One of the men who came in had had eight children in eight years, and the doctor told him that he absolutely had to wear a sheath. He explained that as long as he wore it his woman could not have another baby.

About a month later, the wife came in and she was pregnant. The doctor got very angry. He called the man in and gave him a long lecture through an interpreter.

He asked the man why he hadn't worn the sheath. The interpreter said, "He swears he did wear it. He never took it off." The doctor shook his head. "In that case, ask him how in hell his wife is pregnant again?"

"He says," said the interpreter, "that after six days he had to take a piss so badly that he cut the end off."

ordon was young and he was horny. When he arrived at the Foreign Legion post he was disturbed by the total absence of females on the post.

"Jeepers, creepers!" he said to the sergeant. "Don't you fellows have any sex here?"

"Sure we do," said the sergeant. "It's just that we of the French Foreign Legion have to adapt to our environment."

"I don't understand."

"Well," the sergeant explained, "the camels come every Thursday afternoon at three o'clock."

"Camels!" the young man snorted in disgust. "Huh!"

But by Thursday, he couldn't wait. He stood at the edge of the camp scanning the horizon.

At ten to three, he could see a cloud of dust. It grew larger, and then a herd of about twenty camels came thundering into the camp.

Jordon couldn't wait. Grabbing the first one by the bridle, he quickly began to fuck it.

The sergeant ran up to him. "Private Jordon, what in hell are you doing?"

"Christ, sergeant, it's easy enough to see!'

"No, no, you fool! The camels come to take us to town so we can get the girls!"

Jim Buckley went to a farm to visit his country cousin. He went into the barn to watch the country cousin attach the udders of a cow to the milking machine. The machine went up and down and milk poured out.

Buckley was fascinated. As soon as his country cousin left the barn on some errand, he decided to attach the machine to his penis to see how it would feel.

Two hours later, the country cousin returned to find Buckley lying on the floor and moaning, "Ohhhhhh. Let me out! Let me out!"

"Land's sake," the country cousin exclaimed. "What's goin' on?"

"Can't you see?" Buckley said. "I stuck my prick in your damned machine and turned it on. This is the eighty-seventh time I've come! And I can't seem to turn it off!"

The country cousin scratched his head. "Jim, I'm afraid I can't turn it off either. But don t you worry. We'll feed you and fan you, and the thing's only set for four quarts."

So this elderly couple were sitting in their tiny old water flat on the lower East Side when the husband said, "Doris, we're in bad shape. Inflation has eaten up our Social Security check. The next one isn't due for a week and we've got no money left for food."

"Could I do anything to help?" she asked.

"Yes, ' he said. "I hate to see you do this but it's the only way. You're going to have to go out and hustle."

"Me?" she said. "At the age of sixty-five?"

"It's the only way," he said.

Resigned to the situation, she went out into the warm night.

She came staggering in early the next morning.

"How did you do?" asked the husband.

"Here," she said, "I've got four dollars and ten cents."

"Four dollars and ten cents," he said. "Who gave you the ten cents?"

"Everybody," she said.

Garfield Goldwater made a great deal of money in the men's clothing business in New York. He gave to all the charities, attended all the fancy balls, had his name in Earl Wilson's column twice a week—and still wasn't happy. In fact, he was becoming so depressed that a friend suggested he see a psychiatrist.

The psychiatrist listened and then said: "Look here, Mr. Goldwater. You've made all this money, but your success is meaningless because you don't do anything for pleasure. Isn't there anything at all you've always wanted to do? A childhood fantasy? A juvenile ambition?"

"Well," said Garfield Goldwater a little reluctantly, "when I was a boy I wanted to go into the jungle on a safari. You know, kind of like Tarzan did."

The psychiatrist advised: "If that's what you wanted to do, then do it. Life is short and the grave is deep. Do it, man, and do it now!"

Garfield decided to take the advice. Two days later, he flew to Africa, where he confronted the world's most famous gorilla safari hunter.

Patiently, the safari hunter explained that he'd retired. However, Garfield Goldwater was not easily put off. "Please, Mr. Safari Hunter," he said, "make one more safari. I'll pay anything you ask. I'm a rich man. Money is no object."

The safari hunter was moved. "I've heard of you,"

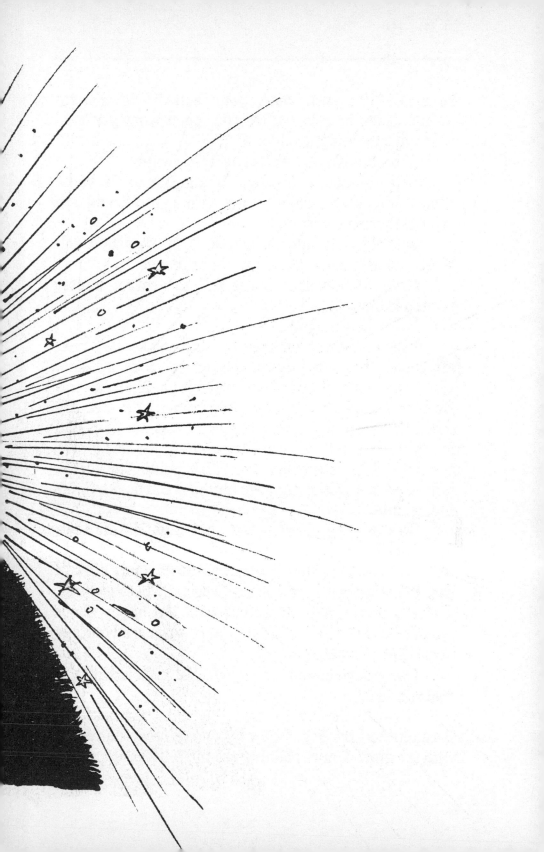

he said. "I've even worn your suits." He thought awhile. Then he asked: "Do you mean what you said about money being no object?"

"Absolutely," vowed Garfield Goldwater.

"All right, here's the deal. In addition to me, you'll need a Zulu, a dog, and a pigmy with a gun. It will cost you ten thousand dollars."

Garfield Goldwater whistled. "Ten thousand dollars!" he exclaimed. "That's a lot of cabbage."

"Only if you don't have it," the safari hunter reminded him.

So Garfield agreed.

The troupe was rounded up, and on the very next afternoon the safari went out on its first mission. Within an hour, the hunter spotted a gorilla in a tree. Everyone stood by while the Zulu climbed the tree. He shook the branches until the gorilla lost his grip and fell to the ground. The dog immediately jumped on the gorilla and bit his penis, at which point the gorilla fainted. A net was slung over him and Garfield had his first gorilla.

He was very pleased. But that night in his tent, Garfield Goldwater thought again about the fee. He went to the safari hunter's tent and awakened him. "I hate to bother you at this hour," he said, "because first, you've done a great job, and second, I'm happy about the gorilla, but third, I think you're taking advantage of me. Ten thousand..."

The safari hunter shrugged. "Mr. Goldwater, a deal is a deal."

"I can understand," said Garfield, "the need for the Zulu and the dog. But why do we need the pigmy with the gun? You're padding the bill a little, old man."

There was no response. The safari hunter had fallen asleep.

The next afternoon, they went out and spotted a larger gorilla in a tree. The Zulu climbed the tree and shook the branches until the gorilla lost his grip and fell to the ground. The dog jumped on the gorilla and bit him on the penis; the gorilla fainted and the safari hunter threw a net over him.

Again Garfield was impressed. But again he began to stew about the high fee. He went to the safari hunter's tent and said: "I want a showdown. I want you to get rid of the pigmy with the gun and reduce my bill."

"Mr. Goldwater," said the safari hunter, "you made a deal. A deal is a deal and that's the deal."

Distraught, Garfield Goldwater returned to his tent. He tried to dream of suits made by Angelo in Rome and ice cream sundaes at Bishoff's in Teaneck, New Jersey, but always his thoughts returned to the ten-thousand-dollar fee and the pigmy with the gun.

The next day, the safari went out, and now it was Garfield Goldwater himself who spotted the gorilla. This time it was a very large one. The Zulu climbed the tree and shook the branches. The Zulu and the gorilla confronted each other, and the two began to wrestle. Suddenly, the gorilla threw the man.

As the Zulu came tumbling down to the ground, he screamed to the pigmy: "Shoot the dog! Shoot the dog!"

Muza Dai Boo, an Arab merchant, was in the marketplace one day when he felt terrible cramps. He just couldn't control himself, and let out a long, loud fart.

People stared at him from all sides. Mortally embarrassed, he ran back to his home, packed his few belongings and journeyed far away. For years he traveled from town to town, but always avoided his home town.

At last, an old and weary man, he decided to return. He had grown a long beard and his face had aged enough so that he was sure he would not be recognized. His heart longed for the old familiar streets.

Once in town, he went directly to the marketplace. There, to his surprise, he saw that the street had been paved. He turned to the man nearest him and said, "My friend, how smooth this street is. When, by the grave of Allah, was it so neatly paved?

"Oh, that," said the man. "That was done three years, four months and two days after Muza Dai Boo farted in the marketplace."

The eighty-eight-year-old millionaire married a four-teen-year-old country girl. He was quite content, but after a few weeks she told him that she was going to leave him if she didn't get some fucking real soon.

He had his chauffeured limousine take him to a high-priced specialist who studied him and then gave him a shot of spermatozoa. "Now look," the doctor said, "The only way you're going to get it hard is to say 'beep,' and then to get it soft again, you say 'beep beep.'"

"How marvelous," the old man said.

"Yes, but I must warn you," the doctor said, "it's only going to work three times before you die."

On his way home, the old man decided he wasn't going to live through three of them anyway, so he decided to waste one trying it out.

"Beep!" he said.

Immediately, his penis got hard.

Satisfied, he said "beep, beep," and his penis got soft again. He chucked with delight and anticipation.

At that moment, a little yellow Volkswagen pulled past his limousine and went "beep," and the car in the opposite lane responded with "beep beep."

Alert to his jeopardy, the old man instructed his chauffeur to "speed it up." He raced into the house as fast as he could for his last great fuck. "Honey," he shouted at her, "don't ask any questions. Just drop your clothes and hop into bed."

Caught up in his excitement, she did. He undressed nervously and hurried in after her. Just as he was climbing into the bed, he said "beep," and his penis leaped to erection.

He was just starting to put it in when his tender young wife said, "What's all this 'beep beep' shit?"

The teacher walked into the classroom to find words like "cunt" and "cock" scrawled all over the blackboard.

"Children," she said, addressing the classroom. "You are much too young to use vile language like that. Now, we're all going to close our eyes and count up to fifty. Then, while our eyes are closed, I want the little boy or girl who wrote those words on the board to tiptoe up and erase them."

At the signal, the teacher and the children all closed their eyes. Then the teacher counted out loud, very slowly.

When she reached fifty, she said, "All right. Everybody open their eyes."

All eyes went to the blackboard.

None of the words were erased. But below them was the message: "Fuck you, teacher. The Phantom strikes again!"

Silas and Sally were out in the cornfield happily fucking away. It had rained that morning and there was lots of mud on the ground, and they found themselves sliding around a bit in the mud.

"Say, honey, is my cock in you or in the mud?" Silas asked.

Sally felt around and said, "Why, Silas, it's in the mud!"

"Well, put it back in you," he said.

After awhile, Silas asked again, "Honey, is it in you or in the mud?"

"In me, honey. In me," Sally cooed happily.

"Well, would you mind putting it back in the mud?"

The teacher told the students that they were going to play a game.

"I've got something behind my back and I'm going to describe it and you guess what it is," she said.

"I'm holding something round and red. Can someone guess?"

"'An apple?" little Herbie said.

"No," said the teacher, "but it shows you were thinking. It's a cherry. Now I'm holding something round and orange. Can you tell me what it is?"

"An orange?" little Herbie said.

"No," said the teacher, "but it shows you were thinking. It's a peach."

Herbie raised his hand. "Teacher, can I play the game too?"

The teacher said yes, and Herbie went to the back of the room, faced the rear and said, "Teacher, I'm holding something about two inches long with a red tip."

The teacher said, "Herbie!"

"No," said little Herbie, "but it shows you were thinking. It's a match."

It happened in Paris in the spring. On a sunny day in May, a Chinaman picked up a whore on the Champs Elysées and took her to the Meurice Hotel.

They opened the windows and the breeze blew in and everything seemed beautiful. The Chinaman got into bed with the whore. He fucked her for awhile and then said, *"Pardonnez-moi, Mademoiselle, je suis fatigué."*

So saying, he went to the window and took a deep breath. Then he went under the bed, came out the other side, and jumped into bed to screw again.

After awhile, he got up saying, *"Pardonnez-moi, Mademoiselle, je suis fatigué."* Again he went to the window, took a deep breath, rolled under the bed and came out the other side.

The sixth time this happened, the whore had become very tired too. Getting out of bed, she said, *"Pardonnez-moi, Monsieur, je suis fatigué."*

She went to the open window, took a deep breath, and looked under the bed. She found four other Chinamen there.

One Friday afternoon, Harold's boss told him that he'd have to work overtime that day. That was okay with Harold except that he had no way of letting his wife know he'd be late coming home, since they had just moved into a new little house in the suburbs and didn't have a phone yet.

"Since I'm passing that way, I'll tell her," the boss volunteered.

A few hours later, the boss arrived at the cottage and rang the doorbell. Harold's wife came to the door wearing a see-through wraparound. The boss couldn't take his eyes off her body.

"Yes?" she said.

"I'm Harold's boss," Harold's boss said. "He's working overtime and asked me to tell you he'll be home late."

"Thank you," she said.

"How about going upstairs for some fucking?"

Harold's wife felt her cheeks flush to an angry red. "How dare you!"

The boss shrugged. "Supposing I give you fifty dollars?"

"Absolutely not! Why, I never heard such nerve...."

"One hundred dollars?"

"Uh...no."

"One hundred and fifty?"

"I don't think that would be right, do you?"

At this point, the boss purred, "Listen, honey, Harold isn't gonna know. It's an easy way to make a hundred and fifty bucks and we'll just spend a little time together."

She nodded, took him by the hand, and led him upstairs to the bed where they had fun and games for an hour.

That night, when Harold came home, he asked, "Did the boss come by to tell you I'd be late?"

"Yes, Harold," the sweet thing said, "he did stop by for a few seconds."

"Good," said Harold. "Then he gave you my salary?"

Benson had been with prostitutes everywhere in the world, but in Hong Kong he met his undoing. He fucked a very sick Chinese whore and picked up so many venereal diseases that the doctors had difficulty separating and identifying them all.

He went to a prominent gynecologist in the American quarter who examined him and shook his head. "Bad news, Benson. You must have immediate surgery and we've got to cut your penis off."

Benson went into traumatic shock at the prognosis. Gathering himself together, he went across the street to another American doctor. There he was told the same thing.

He went out into the street in a daze. Stumbling along, he found himself in the Chinese quarter, where he saw a sign identifying the office of a Chinese surgeon.

Deciding to have one more medical opinion, Benson went in. He told the Chinese doctor that he'd been to two American doctors and both of them wanted to perform immediate surgery to cut off his cock.

The Chinese surgeon examined Benson's penis. He consulted large medical books. Then he examined it again.

"Is there any hope, doc?" Benson asked, plaintively.

"Sure is hope!" the doctor said. "I make complete

79

examination. I know just what's wrong. You play with Chinese girl, but she very sick. You make mistake and go to American doctor. Trouble with American doctors, they always think money, money, money."

Benson brightened up. "You mean I don't need surgery? My penis doesn't have to be cut off?"

"Forget what they say. Go home," the Chinese doctor repeated. "No surgery. Go home. Wait two, maybe three weeks. Pecker fall off all by himself."

A man took his wife to a Broadway show. During the first act intermission, he had to urinate in the worst way. He hurried to the back of the theatre and searched in vain for the men's room.

At last he came upon a fountain surrounded by pretty foliage. He realized that he had wandered backstage. Noting that no one was around, and in desperation, he opened his pants and pissed into the fountain.

He had difficulty finding his way back to the auditorium, and by the time he sat down next to his wife, the curtain was up and actors were moving about on the stage.

"Did I miss much of the second act?" he whispered.

"Miss it?" she said, "You were in it!"

The man was dining in a very swank restaurant in New York City. When the elderly waiter brought the consommé the customer saw that his thumb was deep in the soup bowl.

Next, the waiter served *steak Diane*, and now his thumb was deep in the gravy. The customer held his tongue. This was, after all, one of New York's finest restaurants.

Finally, for dessert, the waiter brought out *coupe marron*. This time his finger was not in the ice cream.

The customer could contain himself no longer. "Sir," he said to the waiter, "would you tell me why you put your finger in the consommé and the steak gravy, but not in the *coupe marron*?"

The waiter stared coldly at him for a moment, and then replied, "Simple, my good man. I have a bad case of arthritis and warm things relieve the pain in my thumb."

The customer became very angry. "You son-of-a-bitch!" he said, "Putting your thumb in my food! You should take that thumb and ram it up your ass!"

The waiter looked at him dourly and said, "That's what I do in the kitchen."

**D**o you know the difference between a cock-
sucker and a corned beef sandwich?
No.
Good. Come over tomorrow for lunch.

The Japanese-American was a long-time customer at this Greek restaurant because he had discovered that they made especially tasty fried rice. Each evening he'd come in he would order "flied lice."

This always caused the Greek restaurant owner to nearly roll on the floor with laughter. Sometimes he'd have two or three friends stand nearby just to hear the Japanese customer order his "flied lice."

Eventually, the customer's pride was so hurt that he took a special diction lesson just to be able to say "fried rice" correctly.

The next time he went to the restaurant, he said very plainly, "Fried rice, please."

Unable to believe his ears, the Greek restaurant owner said, "Sir, would you repeat that?"

The Japanese-American replied: "You heard what I said, you fluckin Gleek!"

The Israeli army unit was crossing the desert and most of the men were on camels. Lt. Smith had a very stubborn camel, and finally it stopped dead in its tracks and refused to move another step.

The rest of the unit moved on, leaving Smith along with his mulish camel.

Smith sat on the camel for three hours. He kicked the camel. He pleaded with the camel. He shouted curses at the camel. But the camel wouldn't move.

He dismounted, and was standing disconsolately at its side when a woman soldier drove up in a jeep. She asked Lt. Smith what the trouble was, and he explained the camel wouldn't budge.

"Oh, I can fix that," she said, jumping out of her jeep. She reached down and put her hand under the camel's belly. The camel jumped up and down, up again, and then suddenly raced away at the rate of half a mile a minute.

Lt. Smith was astounded. "What did you do, lady? What's the trick?"

"It's simple, Lieutenant. I just tickled his balls."

"Well, lady, you'd better tickle mine too, and quickly, because I've got to catch that camel!"

A man was asked by his wife to buy a live chicken for a special dinner. He bought the chicken and was on his way home when he remembered that he didn't have his house key and his wife wouldn't be there for a few hours.

He decided to pass the time by going to a movie. In order to get into the cinema, he stuffed the chicken into his trousers.

He sat down and began watching the movie. It fascinated him so that he didn't notice the chicken sticking its head through his fly.

Two women were sitting next to him, and one of them nudged the other. "Look," she said, "look at that thing there sticking out of the man's pants."

The other replied, "If you've seen one, you've seen them all."

The first one said, "Yes, but this one is eating my popcorn!"

Three nuns were walking along the street and one was describing with her hands the tremendous grapefruit she'd seen in Florida.

The second one, also with her hands, described the huge bananas she'd seen in Jamaica.

The third nun, a little deaf, asked, "Father who?"

So there were these two blacks from a southern town and they wanted women desperately but couldn't find any. They were driving along the country road when they spotted a pig. One of them jumped out, scooped up the pig and stuck it on the seat between them.

They continued to chug along in their 1969 Ford when a police siren suddenly sounded behind them. A glance at the rear view mirror showed them that a police car was in hot pursuit. They pulled over to the side. Not wanting to be caught with a stolen pig, they tossed a blanket over it.

The officer came up to the side of their car. "What are you up to?" he asked.

"We were just out looking for women," one of the lads replied truthfully.

Suddenly the pig stuck its face through the folds of the blanket.

The cop stared, shook his head sadly, and said, "Lady, can you tell me what a nice Southern girl like you is doing with these two Blacks?"

A man was standing on a train platform seeing the train off and he observed someone near him shouting at one of the departing passengers, "Goodbye. Your wife was a great lay! Your wife was a great lay!"

He was stunned.

After the train pulled away, he walked over to the man who'd done the shouting, and asked, "Did I hear you correctly? Did you tell that man his wife was a great lay?"

The other man shrugged his shoulders. "It isn't really true," he said, "but I don't want to hurt his feelings."

The little boy was sitting on the curb crying and an old man who was passing by came over to him.

"What's the matter, little boy?" he asked. "Why are you crying?"

The little boy said, "I'm crying because I can't do what the big boys do."

The old man sat down on the curb and cried too.

Some Americans were touring the marketplace and one of them saw a man on the ground brushing his camel.

"Excuse me, sir," the American said. "Do you know the time?"

The Arab looked at the American. Then he reached over and held the camel's balls, moving them slightly.

"Ten after two," he said, at last.

"My word!" said the American. He caught up to his tour group and insisted some of the others return with him. "You've never seen anything like this!" he promised.

The group went back with him. Again he asked for the time. Again the Arab camel driver reached for the camel's balls. He seemed to be weighing them as he moved them to and fro. Finally, he announced: "Twenty-one minutes past two."

The others were amazed. They went on their way, but the original discoverer of the miracle time-teller remained. He leaned over. "Listen," he confided to the Arab. "I'd give anything to know how you do that. I'll give you twenty American dollars if you show me how you tell the time."

The Arab camel driver thought for a moment, and then nodded. Pocketing the twenty-dollar bill, he beckoned for the American to kneel down where he was.

Then he took the camel's balls and gently moved them to the side, out of the way.

"Do you see that clock over there?" he asked.

He was a junior bank executive and he had swindled one hundred thousand dollars from his bank—all of which he'd lost at the races. The bank examiners were coming the next day, and when he confessed the whole thing to his wife, she packed her bags and left him. Totally despondent, he walked to a nearby bridge and stood at the edge of it about to jump off and end it all.

Suddenly a voice called, "Young man, don't do that! There is no need to end your life! I'm a witch and I can help you!"

"I doubt it," he said sadly, "I've stolen a hundred thousand dollars from the bank, for which I'll probably be arrested tomorrow, and my wife has left me."

"Young man, witches can do anything," she said. "I'm going to perform a witch miracle." She said, "*Alakazam!* the hundred thousand dollars has been replaced and there's another hundred thousand in your safe deposit box! *Alakazam!* Your wife is back home again!"

He looked at her in disbelief, "Is this all true?" he asked.

"Of course," she said, "but to keep it true you must do one thing."

"Anything!" he said, "Anything!"

"You must take me to a motel and have sexual intercourse with me."

He stared at her. She was an ugly old crone, dressed in rags. Nevertheless, he agreed to her terms. He took her to a motel and screwed her all night. In the morning, as he was getting dressed and combing his hair in front of the mirror, she lay on the bed watching silently. Finally, she asked, "Sonny, how old are you?"

"I'm thirty-two," he said.

"Tell me something, then," she said. "Aren't you a little too old to believe in witches?"

It was his wedding night and the minister finished undressing in the bathroom and walked into the bedroom. He was surprised to see that his bride had already slipped between the bed sheets.

"My dear," he said, "I thought I would find you on your knees."

She said, "Well, honey, I can do it that way too, but it gives me the hiccoughs."

The newly-married Italian couple came home to Brooklyn from their honeymoon and moved into the upstairs apartment they'd rented from the groom's parents.

That night, the father of the groom was awakened from his deep sleep by his wife nudging him by hitting his stomach with her elbow. "Tony, listen!" she whispered.

He listened. Upstairs, the bed was creaking in rhythm.

The wife said, "Come on, Tony!" So Tony rolled on top of her and fucked her.

He was trying to fall back to sleep when, fifteen minutes later, the same sounds were heard. The wife said, "Tony! Listen to them! Come on, Tony!"

Once again, Tony got on top of her and fucked her.

A short time later, the bedsprings upstairs began to squeak again. And again the wife nudged her husband. "Tony, listen!" At this, Tony leaped from the bed, grabbed a broom, and banged the handle against the ceiling as he shouted, "Hey, kids, cut it out! You're killing your old man!"

So this husband from Roslyn Heights, Long Island, kissed his wife goodbye and got into his Cadillac to drive to work in New York City. He'd gone about a mile when he remembered that he'd left something in the bedroom. So he turned the car around and drove back home.

When he walked into the bedroom, there was his wife, lying totally nude on the bed and the milkman standing totally nude beside her.

The milkman promptly went into a squatting position on the rug and said, "I'm glad you're here, Mr. Jones, because I was just telling your wife that if she doesn't pay the milk bill, I'm gonna shit all over the floor."

A man who was very depressed met his friend, Jerry J., who was a very sharp thinker.

"What's the matter?" Jerry J. asked.

"I'm despondent. I can't adjust to the fact that I've got three balls."

"Three balls?" said sharp Jerry. "Kid, we can make a fortune together!"

"How?" asked the other fellow, brightening up.

"We'll go to bar after bar and bet everybody around that between you and the bartender you've got five balls! It can't miss!"

"Let's go," said the man.

So they went into the first bar, and Jerry J. made friends with the strangers at the bar. Then he made the announcement: "I'll bet anybody in the place that between my friend here and the bartender they've got five balls."

Nearly everyone rushed forward to cover the bet.

Jerry looked at the bartender who was shaking his head.

"You don't mind being part of the wager, do you?" Jerry asked.

"Not at all," the bartender said. "I'm very impressed."

"How do you mean?" Jerry asked.

"Well, up to now I've never met a man with four balls. I've only got one."

young farm boy from Arkansas was sent to New York by his father to learn the undertaking business under the tutelage of the great Frank E. Campbell.

Some months later, the father visited his son in the big city. "Tell me," he said, "have you learned much?"

"Oh sure, Dad," said the son. I've learned a lot. And it's been very interesting."

"What was the most interesting thing you learned?"

The son thought for a minute and then said, "Well, we did have one wild experience that taught me a lesson."

"What was that?"

"Well," said the son, "one day we got this phone call from the Taft Hotel. It seems that the housekeeper had checked one of the rooms and she discovered that a man and woman had died in their sleep on the bed and completely naked."

"Wow!" said the father. "What did Mr. Campbell do?"

"Well, he put on his tuxedo and he had me put on my tuxedo. Then we were driven in one of his limousines to the Taft Hotel. The manager took us to the desk clerk who gave us the room number. Then the manager rode up with us in the elevator. We were silent because Mr. Campbell always believed in doing things with great dignity."

"How marvelous!" exclaimed the father. "Then what happened?"

"Well, we came to this room. Mr. Campbell pushed the door open with his gold tipped cane. He, the manager, and I walked in quietly. Sure enough, there on the bed was this naked couple lying on their backs."

"And then what happened?" asked the father.

"Well, Mr. Campbell saw an immediate problem. The man had a large erection."

"And then what happened?" asked the father.

"Mr. Campbell, as usual, was up to the situation He swung his gold-tipped cane and very stylishly whacked the penis."

"And then what happened?" asked the father.

"Well, Dad," said the son, "all hell broke loose. You see, we were in the wrong room!"

The Mother Superior in the convent school was chatting with her young charges and she asked them what they wanted to be when they grew up.

A twelve-year-old said, "I want to be a prostitute."

The Mother Superior fainted dead away on the spot. When they revived her, she raised her head from the ground and gasped, "What—did—you—say—?"

The young girl shrugged. "I said I want to be a prostitute."

"A prostitute!" the Mother Superior said, "Oh, praise sweet Jesus! And I thought you said you wanted to be a Protestant."

Little Jimmy had become a real nuisance while the men tried to concentrate on their Saturday afternoon poker game. His father tried in every way he could to get Jimmy to occupy himself, but the youngster insisted on running back and forth behind the players and calling out the cards they held.

The players became so annoyed that they threatened to quit the game. At this point, the boy's uncle stood up, took Jimmy by the hand, and led him out of the room. The uncle returned in a short time without Jimmy and without comment, and the game resumed.

For the balance of the afternoon, there was no trouble from Jimmy. After the game had ended and the players were settling their wins and losses, one of the men asked Jimmy's uncle, "What in the world did you do to Jimmy?"

"Not much," the boy's uncle replied. "I showed him how to jerk off."

The bridegroom carried his bride over the threshold and into the honeymoon suite. They had taken off all their clothes, when suddenly the sweet young thing began to tremble.

"What's the matter, honey?" he asked in a concerned voice.

She was now shivering all over. "I've got an attack of St. Vitus Dance," she said.

The groom thought about it for a minute, then picked up the hotel phone and called the bell captain for help.

Four bellboys came rushing into the room.

"Quick! You grab her arms," the young man shouted to two of them. To the other two, he directed, "Grab her legs and hold her tight."

He leaped into the bed on top of her, inserted his penis into her, and then shouted to the straining bellboys, "Okay, fellows, let her go!"

A Frenchman who was leaving his home in Paris for a few weeks confided in his friend, Pierre: "I always hate to leave the city. When I'm away, I just don't know what my wife is doing. There's always the doubt, always the doubt."

Pierre said, "Charles, I'll tell you what. Because we're such good friends, I'll keep an eye on her every evening that you're gone."

"Would you do that for me?" Charles said, obviously delighted and relieved. He kissed Pierre on both cheeks. "You understand, dear friend, that I know I should trust my wife. It's just that there's always the doubt, always the doubt."

"Have no fear, Pierre will be there," the friend said.

Three weeks later, Charles returned to Paris and the two men met.

"Charles, I'm afraid I have bad news for you," Pierre said.

"Well?"

"The very first night you were gone, I watched this man go to your house. Your wife opened the door and kissed and hugged him. He fondled her breast. He rubbed her crotch. Then they closed the door to go upstairs. Never daunted, I climbed the tree outside your house and I observed them closely from one of its branches."

"And so—?" said Charles.

"Well, first they took off all their clothes. Incidentally, dear friend, your wife has a lovely body."

"She does, indeed," said Charles thoughtfully. "What happened then?"

"Then?" Pierre shook his head sorrowfully. "Then is when they turned out the lights. I could see nothing. I could learn nothing more."

Charles sighed a deep sigh. "So you see how it is, my friend? Always the doubt, always the doubt."

Two factory workers were at their lathes and one of them said, "Listen, are you going to the hockey game tomorrow night? You know, it's the big game. The Rangers are playing Montreal."

"Naw," said the other one, "my wife won't let me go."

"You're a fool. There's nothing to it."

"What do you mean?"

"Well, an hour before the game you simply pick her up, carry her to the bed, fling her on the bed, tear off her clothes, fuck her, and say, 'I'm going to the hockey game'!"

The following Monday, the two men met at work and the first one said, "What happened? I didn't see you at the game. Didn't you do what I suggested?"

The second man said: "I'll tell you how it was. An hour before the game, I picked up the wife, carried her to the bedroom, and flung her onto the bed."

"Yes?"

"And then, just as I was pulling off her panties and opening my fly, I thought to myself, what the hell, Montreal hasn't been playing that well lately."

The judge came home and found his wife in bed with his very best friend.

"Hey, what do you think you're doing?"

"See," the wife said to the man beside her, "I told you he was stupid."

This seedy looking girl walked into a seedy looking bar. A couple of seeding looking customers stood at the other end.

"Gimme a Rheingold," she said.

She took the glass of beer and swallowed it with one gulp. Then she fell to the floor in a dead faint.

"Come, give me a hand," the bartender called. The two men helped the bartender carry her into the back room. One of the men glanced around and said, "Listen. Nobody'll know. How about we all give her a quick fuck?"

They did just that. An hour or so later, she came to and said, "Where am I? What time is it? I've got to get home." And out she went.

Next afternoon, there were six men hanging around the bar when the same girl came in, walked up to the bartender and said, "Gimme a Rheingold."

She drank it down in one gulp and then fell to the floor in a dead faint.

The men carried her to the back room and the fucking performance was repeated, except that now there were seven, including the bartender.

The next day when she came in, there were twenty-four men, all waiting around.

"Gimme a Rheingold," she said. She swallowed it in one gulp, fell to the floor in a dead faint, and was carried to the back room, where all twenty-four men partook of her.

When she arrived on the fourth day, the word had really gotten around, and there were more than seventy men in the bar. waiting eagerly with lustful eyes and eager cocks. As the walked up to the bar. the bartender pushed a glass of beer toward her.

"You want your Rheingold, Miss?" she said.

"No," she said. "You better give me a Schlitz. That Rheingold gives me a pain in the cunt."

He was very wealthy and very old—in fact, he was about to celebrate his eighty-third birthday. He went to the doctor for a checkup. The doctor gave him a thorough going-over, and then said, "For a man who's about to be eighty-three, you're in marvelous shape. But why a physical just a day before your birthday?"

The wealthy old man explained that that very afternoon he was going to marry an eighteen-year-old girl.

The doctor tried with a great deal of effort to dissuade him. "I'm goin' ahead with it no matter what," the old man said. "Got any other suggestions, Doc?"

"Just one. If you want a really peaceful marriage, I suggest that you take in a boarder."

The old man thought about it and said that it sounded like a good idea.

The next time the doctor met the old man it was at a fund-raising affair, half a year later. The old man came up to him and said, "Doctor, congratulate me! My wife's pregnant!"

The doctor tried to maintain his poise, and said, "Well, so at least you followed my good advice and took in a boarder."

"Oh, sure," said the old man, with a wicked grin, "and the boarder's pregnant as well!"

Once upon a time there was a sperm named Stanley who lived inside a famous movie actor. Stanley was a very healthy sperm. He'd do push-ups and somersaults and limber himself up all the time, while the other sperm just lay around on their fat asses not doing a thing.

One day, one of them became curious enough to ask Stanley why he exercised all day.

Stanley said, "Look, pal, only one sperm gets a woman pregnant and when the right time comes, I am going to be that one."

A few days later, they all felt themselves getting hotter and hotter, and they knew that it was getting to be their time to go. They were released abruptly and, sure enough, there was Stanley swimming far ahead of all the others.

All of a sudden, Stanley stopped, turned around, and began to swim back with all his might. "Go back! Go back!" he screamed. "It's a blow job!"

He was on his way home when he came upon a woman crying hysterically. "What's the matter, lady?" he asked.

She could only sob, "Schultz is dead. Schultz is dead!"

He shook his head and continued walking. Suddenly he came upon another woman sobbing, "Schultz is dead, Schultz is dead!"

He couldn't get over it because soon he came upon another woman crying the same thing. He had never seen so many unhappy women. And then he came upon a scene that caused him to stop. A trolley car had run over a man and had cut him into pieces. There, on the pavement next to the body, was this foot-and-a-half-long penis, and a half-dozen women were standing around crying hysterically, "Schultz is dead. Schultz is dead!"

When he arrived home, he greeted his wife with, "I just saw the damndest thing. A trolley car ran over a man and cut off his cock, and would you believe it, the cock was a foot and a half long."

"Oh my God!" the wife screamed, "Schultz is dead. Schultz is dead!"

Marilyn had a parrot for a pet, but the parrot would embarrass her whenever she came into the apartment with a man. He would shout all kinds of obscenities, always leading off with "Somebody's gonna get it tonight! Somebody's gonna get it tonight!"

In desperation, Marilyn went to her local pet shop and explained her parrot problem to the pet shop proprietor.

"What you need," he said, "is a female parrot too. I don't have one on hand, but I'll order one. Meanwhile, you could borrow this female owl until the female parrot arrives."

Marilyn took the owl home and put it near her parrot. It was immediately obvious that the parrot didn't care for the owl. He glared at it.

The night, Marilyn wasn't her usual nervous self as she opened the door to bring her gentleman friend in for a nightcap. Then suddenly she heard the parrot screech and she knew that things hadn't changed.

"Somebody's gonna get it tonight! Somebody's gonna get it tonight!" the parrot said.

The owl said, "Whooo? Whooo?

And the parrot said, "Not you, you big-eyed son-of-a-bitch!"

Mr. "J"

More of The World's Best Dirty Jokes

Illustrations by TED ENIK

Foreword

The stories and jokes in this collection are part and parcel of the folklore of America.

They are printed as they have been told, by word of mouth. In other times these jokes would have been subjected to stringent editing. Fortunately, today's mores permit almost limitless freedom of expression.

And we are all the richer for it.

Allen was sitting at a bar in a Miami Beach hotel feeling exceedingly horny, when a beautiful prostitute approached him.

"How much do you want?" asked Allen.

"One hundred dollars for the evening," said the prostitute.

"Well, if I'm going to pay that kind of money, you must do it under my rules."

She said, "Honey, that's fine, as long as you're paying."

Allen said, "Okay, meet me in my room in ten minutes and we'll close the drapes, turn out the lights, and do it in pitch-black darkness."

"That's okay, honey. It's your money."

When they got together in the room, Allen really gave it to her. Then he said, "Let's rest a few moments," and then he started in again. The same scene was played for two hours. Finally, after six encounters, Allen seemed even stronger than before.

The prostitute said, "Allen you are the most fantastic lover I have ever had. You just keep getting better and better."

"Listen, lady," said a voice. "My name is Herman. Allen is outside selling your ass to his friends at fifty bucks a throw."

Definition of a diaphragm: a trampoline for schmucks.

As Adam wandered about the Garden of Eden, he noticed two birds up in a tree. They were snuggled up together, billing and cooing.

Adam called to the Lord, "What are the two birds doing in the trees?"

The Lord said, "They are making love, Adam."

A little while later he wandered into the fields and saw a bull and a cow going at it hot and heavy. He called to the Lord, "Lord, what's going on with that bull and cow?"

And the Lord said, "They're making love, Adam."

Adam said, "How come I don't have anyone to make love with?"

So the Lord said, "We'll change that. When you awake tomorrow morning things will be different."

So Adam lay down beneath the olive tree and fell asleep. When he awoke, there was Eve next to him. Adam jumped up, grabbed her hand, and said, "Come with me. Let's go into the bushes." And so they went.

But a few moments later Adam stumbled out, looking very dejected, and called to the Lord, "Lord, what's a headache?"

A New York dress manufacturer, specializing in the production of pastel dresses, had signs pasted in the washrooms: YOU ARE WORKING ON PASTELS! EMPLOYEES MUST WASH HANDS AFTER USING THE LAVATORY.

Two workers, buttoning their flies as they emerged from the washroom, were queried by the boss: "Did you wash your hands? You're working on pastels."

"Nah," replied one worker. "We're not working on pastels. We're going to lunch!"

A patient at Mount Sinai Hospital, recovering from minor surgery, was being given an alcohol rubdown by two of the hospital's more attractive nurses. While manipulating the man's body they noted that the word *tiny* was tattooed on the head of his penis.

Some months after the man's discharge, Mary, one of the nurses, told Joan, the other, that she had dated their former patient.

"How could you go out with a man who had 'tiny' tattooed on his love stick?" exclaimed Joan.

"How could I indeed!" said Mary. "It said 'tiny' when it was quiet, but when I aroused it, it spelled out 'Tiny's Delicatessen and Catering Service. We deliver at all times, twenty-four hours a day!'"

An inventor, seeking a loan from a bank, told his banker that he'd discovered a remarkable substance that, brushed lightly over a lady's pussy, would give it an orange flavor.

"No good," the banker responded, after some thought. "But if you can invent something to put into an orange that will make it taste like pussy, you can have your loan and we'll both get rich!"

Ashy young man, preparing himself for what he hoped would be the ultimate sex act with a pretty young lady, went into a drugstore to inquire about sizes and styles of condoms.

The lusty proprietress, a buxom widow, saw an opportunity for fun at the lad's expense.

"Come in the back and try some on for size," she said, taking his hand. The widow unzipped the youth's fly and watched the small instrument grow in her hand as she measured it. When the weapon had unfurled to a rosy seven and a half inches, the young man, unable to contain himself, had an orgasm with a tremendous discharge. After recovering, he asked the widow if she could now give him the proper size.

"I'll do more than that," she said. "I'll give you free meals and a one-half interest in the store."

I'm so tired," complained the pretty young actress to her friend. "Last night I didn't sleep until after three."

"No wonder you're tired," her friend replied. "Twice is usually all I need."

A happily married man, Irving Topper, found himself driving through a badly paved country road in upstate Rhinebeck, New York. A sudden flat tire sent the car wobbling to a standstill.

The lights in a nearby health manor invited Topper to rap on the door. An attractive lady opened the door and asked what she could do for him. He told her his problem and wondered if he could seek the shelter of her house until dawn, when he would repair the flat. The lady agreed and invited him into her parlor.

One word led to another; one drink led to another; one touch led to another. Irving Topper was soon divested of his clothes and snuggling in the lady's bed with an equally naked lady.

In the morning Topper thanked her for her hospitality, told her his name was Herman Thompson, changed his tire, and drove off.

About six months later, Topper received a call from his friend Herman Thompson.

"Hey," said Thompson, "did you ever give my name to a lady in Rhinebeck, New York?"

"Well, yes," answered Topper. "You know I am a married man, and I have a lovely wife and child. I gave her your name because you're a bachelor, and I didn't want any complications. I hope I didn't get you into any trouble."

"No, no, on the contrary," replied his friend. "Her

lawyer called me to inform me that I had inherited the manor and the lady's entire estate!"

A painter, whitewashing the inner walls of a country outhouse, had the misfortune to fall through the opening and land in the muck at the bottom. He shouted, "Fire! Fire! Fire!" at the top of his lungs.

The local fire department responded with alacrity, sirens roaring as they approached the privy.

"Where's the fire?" called the chief.

"No fire," replied the painter as they pulled him out of the hole. "But if I had yelled, 'Shit! Shit! Shit!' who would have rescued me?"

A seventy-five-year-old gentleman visited his doctor to complain about his impotency.

"Why me?" he grumbled. "I have a friend eighty years old who says that he—"

The doctor interrupted: "You can *say* too!"

Bendelman, a top salesman for a wholesale hardware company, was traveling on one of his quarterly selling swings. When he arrived in Indianapolis he was caught in a blizzard of awesome proportions. At the end of the day he was happy to seek the warmth of his hotel room. One of his major accounts found the snow so heavy that he felt he could not drive to his suburban home. He asked Bendelman if he could put him up for the night in his room, since the hotel was full.

Bendelman, knowing that the man was one of his best accounts, glady offered to share his double-bedded room. After a good dinner and ample liquor they repaired for the night. In the middle of the night Bendelman felt a hand on his privates. Possibly his companion was dreaming. But there was no mistaking his intent when an erect penis brushed against his lips.

When Bendelman returned home he told his wife the story. "And what did you do?" she asked.

"What could I do?" sighed Bendelman. "He was my best account in Indianapolis."

An eminent teacher and thinker once expressed his philosophy of life succinctly. "When it all boils down to the essence of truth," the philosopher said, "one must live by a dog's rule of life: If you can't eat it or fuck it, piss on it!"

A.____ B.____ C.____

The young farm helper was telling his friend about his wedding night.

"Boy, was my girl dumb! She put a pillow under her ass instead of her head."

wo friends decided they would beat the draft by having all their teeth pulled. They knew the army would not take them if they were toothless.

Finally the day came when they were to report to the draft board. As they lined up they were separated by a big truck driver who obviously had not bathed for weeks. When the first friend stood before the sergeant for a physical examination he told the sergeant that he had no teeth. The sergeant ran his fingers around the man's gums and said, "All right, you have no teeth— you're 4F."

Next came the big, smelly truck driver. The sergeant said, "What's wrong with you?"

The truck driver replied, "I have a terrible case of piles."

The sergeant inserted his fingers in the truck driver's ass, felt around, and said, "Yes, indeed you do; you're 4F."

Next came the second friend, and the sergeant said, "What's wrong with you?"

The recruit stared at the sergeant's finger. "Nothing, Sergeant," he said. "Nothing at all."

Mrs. Anderson's husband had been reported missing for more than three months. Her friends and relatives did not know if the poor man had met with foul play or had merely absented himself from the family hearth.

One day the lady received a call from the city morgue requesting her to identify a body that might very well be Mr. Anderson.

The morgue attendant lifted the sheet, disclosing the recently dead but very well-endowed corpse.

"No," Mrs. Anderson said. "That isn't my husband, but some woman certainly lost a very good friend."

**M**arty was walking down the street when he saw his friend and yelled to him, "John, how are you?"

John replied, "Don't call me John. Call me Lucky."

"Why should I call you Lucky?"

John proceeded to tell him that he had been standing on the corner of 52nd Street and Third Avenue, when he stepped off the curb just as a two-ton safe fell from the twentieth floor. It landed right where he had been standing an instant earlier.

Marty said, "My God, you certainly are lucky. That will be your name from now on."

A few weeks later they bumped into each other again, and Marty said, "Lucky, how are you?"

To which came the reply, "Don't call me Lucky. Call me Lucky, Lucky."

Marty said, "Tell me now, why I should call you Lucky, Lucky?" and was told that Lucky had been bumped from a flight to Miami that was later hijacked to Cuba.

Marty agreed, "You certainly are Lucky, Lucky."

The next time they met, Marty shouted, "Lucky, Lucky, how are you?"

To which the reply was, "Don't call me Lucky, Lucky. Call me Lucky, Lucky, Lucky."

Marty said, "Why?"

Lucky, Lucky, Lucky said, "Just last week I took

my girlfriend to a hotel room for a matinee, and we made such a commotion that the chandelier over the bed came down and landed right on her cunt."

Marty said, "But what's so lucky about that?"

To which came the reply, "Ten seconds earlier, it would have cut off my head."

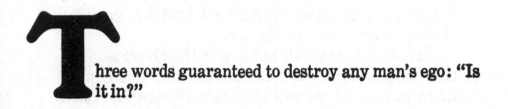hree words guaranteed to destroy any man's ego: "Is it in?"

The Pope had been sick for a number of months, and experts were called in from all over the world, but no one could diagnose his illness. Finally a doctor from Switzerland came and immediately hit upon the cause of the problem.

He said to the Pope, "Your Holiness, because you have lived in a celibate state all your life, your seminal fluids have built up and are literally choking you to death. Therefore, there is only one cure. You must have sexual intercourse with a woman!"

The Pope cried out in dismay, "But I can't. I *can't!* You know the vows I have taken. I just cannot."

The doctor replied, "But Your Holiness, if you don't do this you will condemn yourself to death. This, too, is a mortal sin."

The Pope pondered the problem and said, "I will retire to my room for three days of prayer, and then I will make a decision."

At the end of the three days he telephoned the doctor in Switzerland and said, "My decision has been made. I will do what you direct. But please be sure that she has big tits!"

A young whore, after banging some thirty men in the course of the evening, died and was taken to the great Olympia in the sky. There she met the god Thor, who immediately made a pass at her.

"You cannot reject me," he exclaimed. "I'm Thor!"

"*You're* thor," she mimicked. "After thirty guys in a row, I'm the one who's sore!"

A father was talking to his son just before the son's marriage, explaining what the son could be looking forward to in his marriage.

He said, "Son, in the very beginning, it's tri-weekly. After you've been married ten years or so, it's try weekly. But then after your silver anniversary, it's try weakly."

The priest at Sunday mass noticed that Michael took a ten-dollar bill and two one-dollar bills from the collection plate, instead of putting something in. He thought to himself, *I'd better watch out for Michael.*

The next week he noticed the same thing. So he waited outside church when mass was over, and as Michael came out, he accosted him and said, "Michael, tell me—why did you take out a ten-dollar bill and two singles two weeks in a row, instead of putting money into the collection?"

Michael replied, "Father, I'm embarrassed, but I did it because I needed a blow job."

The priest looked surprised but said to Michael, "Listen, don't do that any more. I'll be watching you from now on."

When he got back to the rectory, the priest was still perplexed. Finally he decided to call Mother Agatha at the convent. He said, "Mother, you've been such a great friend of mine, I have a question for you. What is a blow job?"

Mother Agatha replied, "Oh, about twelve dollars."

The famous Yiddish actor Boris Tomashefsky was celebrated for his bedroom exploits as well as his stage virtuosity. After a sexual bout with a local whore, he presented her with a pair of tickets to the evening performance of his play.

The lady looked with skepticism at the tickets. "With these you can buy bread?" she asked.

"If you're looking for bread," the actor said, "screw a baker."

A husband, returning home unexpectedly, found his wife on her hands and knees scrubbing the kitchen floor. The piston-like movement of her buttocks, encased in a sheer dressing gown, sent a message to his brain.

Without a by-your-leave, he lifted her gown, unzipped himself, and proceeded to mount her.

After they had sighed in mutual satisfaction, the wife resumed her task. This time he booted her in the behind.

"Is that nice, Sam, kicking me after I gave you so much pleasure?"

"That," he said, "is for not looking to see who it was!"

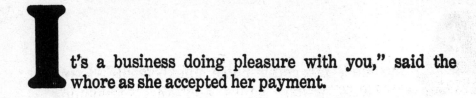

It's a business doing pleasure with you," said the whore as she accepted her payment.

LM. Goldman, a traveling representative for a
brush company, covered the entire eastern seaboard. Each day he would send the home office an itemized column of expenses for that day. He would list food, transportation, and hotel charges, and at the bottom of each page of expenditures he would add, "5.00—a man isn't made of wood."

When the home office received seven consecutive similar notations they cabled Goldman: "It's true a man isn't made of wood, but he isn't made of steel, either!"

A whore and her pimp were lounging in her hotel room, when she got a call from a customer. The pimp, despite the frigid weather outside, offered to wait out on the balcony while the whore did her work.

The customer turned up in ten minutes and was soon humping the whore under the warm blanket. A half hour later, refreshed and satisfied, the customer left.

The pimp, shivering, his lips blue from the biting cold and icicles on his ears, returned to the room and called, "Has that sucker gone yet?"

A man, very much on the make for his secretary, wined her and dined her. He finally succeeded in getting her to his apartment, where he whispered sweet promises into her ear while he began to unbutton her blouse.

"If we get together," he said, "a fur coat . . . perhaps a trip to Europe."

The secretary nodded a cheerful agreement, and soon the two were locked in intercourse. Later, while dressing, she asked him when she could get the fur coat he'd promised.

"What fur coat?" he asked.

"You promised me a fur coat," she said.

"When I'm horny I'll promise anything," he said. Putting one hand on his heart and one on his sexual organ, he added, "When he's soft, he's hard. When he's hard, he's soft."

Jessie James and his gang attacked a train just outside Oklahoma City. They went through each car lining up the travelers and preparing to take all the loot they could handle.

Jessie entered the first car and yelled, "Okay, everybody, we're going to rape all the men and rob all the women."

His brother Frank turned to him and said, "Jessie, we're going to rob all the men and rape all the women."

With that, a little fairy in the corner piped up, "Listen, you heard Jessie. He's the boss."

Ayoung salesman visited a whorehouse in Kansas City and proceeded to give the blonde prostitute the greatest lay she had ever experienced.

"Listen," she said, "if you can repeat that performance, I'll give it to you for nothing."

The salesman said, "Okay, but let me rest for ten minutes. But while I do, to help recharge my batteries, just sit here and hold my cock." After ten minutes, he gave it to her again, and it was more wonderful than the first time.

When they were through, the excited prostitute said, "Please, let's do it again. You can have it for nothing."

The salesman said, "Okay, just give me another ten-minute rest and sit here holding my cock."

She said, "Of course." Then she said, "Listen, I can understand your wanting that ten-minute rest, but why do you have me sit here holding your cock?"

"Because in St. Louis, the last prostitute I visited stole my wallet!"

Then there's the story of the man who was standing on Delancey Street gazing at his watch, which was obviously not working. He spied a corner shop which had a gigantic clock in the window. Thinking it was a watch-repair shop, he approached the owner and said, "My watch doesn't work; please fix it for me."

The owner said, "I'm not a watchmaker. I'm a *mohel.*"*

The man replied, "Then why do you have the big clock in your window?"

Said the shopkeeper, "What would you put in your window?"

* *Mohel:* Yiddish, one who circumcises.

The famous stage magician had a thundering climax to his act. He would fill a large bowl with shit and proceed to slurp it noisily, to the amazement and delight of the audience.

One evening he had just begun the wow finish of the act when he stopped in his tracks.

"Go ahead," murmured the stage manager. "Eat the shit. Eat it!"

"Can't do it," said the magician. "There's a hair in it!"

The bride-to-be and her best friend were discussing the former's impending wedding.

"If you want an unforgettable wedding night," her friend said, "get him to eat a dozen oysters after the ceremony."

A week later the new bride thanked her friend but said plaintively, "Only eight of the oysters worked."

An American soldier, on the train from London to Liverpool, shared a compartment with two English brothers, one of whom was hard of hearing. They struck up a conversation, and one brother said, "I say, Yank, where are you going?"

"Liverpool," said the American.

"What did he say?" asked the hard-of-hearing brother.

"He said he's going to Liverpool. Tell me, Yank, what brings you all the way to Liverpool?"

"I have a girlfriend up there."

"What did he say?" asked the hard-of-hearing brother again.

"He said he has a girlfriend there. She must be quite a girl if you'll travel all the way there just to see her."

"I'll say she is!" said the American. "She wears black boots with spurs, carries a whip, and indulges in every delight known to man."

"What did he say?" asked the brother who was hard of hearing.

"He said he knows Mother."

The Smiths had been married long enough for the bloom to be off the rose. Yet from time to time Smith was overcome by the primal urge. On one such occasion, while they were sitting in the living room before the television set, Smith nudged his wife and said, "How about going into the bedroom?"

"No," said Mrs. Smith.

Smith finally persuaded her to change her mind She disrobed for bed and donned a long nightgown.

"Pull up the nightgown, honey," he requested.

"No," said Mrs. Smith.

Just then the front-door bell rang, and Smith pulled on a robe to answer it. Mrs. Smith immediately leaped from the bed and bolted the bedroom door.

The irate Smith banged on the door and yelled, "Let me in . . . let me in! If you don't unlock the door, I'll break it down."

"Look at him," Mrs. Smith said. "He can't even lift a nightgown, and he's talking about breaking down doors!"

It's very simple," explained the go-go dancer. "First I kick my right foot; then I kick my left foot. Between the two of them, I make a living."

In the romantic days of Warsaw, Viennese whores were known for their beauty and delicacy. A gallant officer picked up one such lady of the evening, who took him to her apartment. They made delicious love all evening before drifting to sleep in each other's arms. In the morning the man dressed, staring into a full-length mirror. The lady lay in her bed watching him.

Finally she said softly, "Didn't you forget something?"

"What did I forget?" asked the officer.

"You forgot about money," said the lady.

"Oh, no," said the man, standing at ramrod attention. "A Polish officer never takes money."

Tom's dream was to marry a sweet, innocent virgin. He'd been going with Jane for a few months, when he decided to test her. As they drove along in the car, he unzipped his fly, turned to her, and said, "Do you want to see my wee-wee?"

She yelled, "No! No! Please zip up your fly."

Instead of being annoyed, Tom was pleased.

On the evening of their engagement to be married, he tried the same thing, with the same result. Finally, on their wedding night, they were alone in the hotel room when he unzipped his fly and said to her, "Darling, now you can look at what I've got here," and proceeded to take out his organ.

She looked at it and replied, "Oh, what a sweet looking wee-wee!"

Tom said, "No, darling—you don't have to call it a wee-wee now; you can call it a cock."

She looked at it for a while and then said, "No, Tom, that's a wee-wee. A cock is long and thick and black."

What are the two most conceited things in the world?

One is the flea, floating down the river on his back with an erection, yelling for the man to raise the drawbridge.

The other is the flea's brother who, after sexually attacking a rhinoceros, whispers in her ear, "Did I hurt you, baby?"

And then there's the little boy who got up at midnight to go to the bathroom and passed his parents' bedroom. Noticing that the door was opened, he walked in and saw his mother performing fellatio on his father.

The boy walked out of the bedroom scratching his head and muttering, "And they sent *me* to the doctor for sucking my thumb!"

The eminent physician was at a loss on how to proceed with treatment for his hypochondriac patient. The man had been consulting with him for months; yet the doctor could find nothing wrong with him.

Finally, the doctor decided to bring matters to a head. This time he gave the patient a large bowl and ordered him to urinate in it. The patient followed orders. Then the doctor ordered him to defecate in the urine. It was difficult but the patient complied.

The physician took a large wooden ladle from a drawer and mixed the concoction. Then he ordered the patient to open his mouth and swallow a large ladleful of the muck. The patient did so and promptly vomited.

"Ah!" said the doctor. "Upset stomach!"

A businessman returned home from the office with some startling gossip. He informed his wife that he'd heard that their neighbor in apartment 4-G had fucked every woman in the building except one.

"That's right," replied the wife. "It's that stuck-up Mrs. Cohen on the eighth floor!"

The parlormaid in the home of a famous acting family was openly desired and admired by the nineteen-year-old son of the household. He schemed and schemed but could think of no way to get the young woman into his bed.

Finally, one evening, opportunity presented itself and he persuaded the young miss to join him between the sheets. Much to his despair and chagrin, his weapon refused to come to attention.

"Don't feel too bad," the parlormaid said. "The same thing often happens to your father."

The Adamses, celebrating their twenty-fifth wedding anniversary, decided to recapture their nuptial night by making love the way they had when they first discovered sex with each other. Mr. Adams perspired until he achieved a serviceable erection, and then began to put it to its proper use.

Mrs. Adams, bouncing under her husband's weight, never took her eyes off the window.

"Darling," she murmured, just as he felt the tickle of approaching orgasm, "should we redo this room with cream curtains or a pretty print?"

Bumper stickers observed:

MECHANICS HAVE THE BEST TOOLS.
LOVE THE NAVY—EAT A SAILOR TODAY!
DON'T BE HALF-GAY.
SMILE . . . IF YOU WERE LAID LAST NIGHT!
JOURNALISTS DO IT EVERY DAY.

 he absent-minded professor unbuttoned his vest, took out his necktie, and wet his pants.

John had two pet monkeys whom he loved very much, but both died within two days of each other. He decided to take their bodies to the taxidermist so that they would be with him forever. The taxidermist gave him an estimate for the job and asked if he wanted them mounted.

"No," came the reply. "Just have them shaking hands."

A young black guy, traveling cross-country with his girlfriend, left her alone in a hotel room while he visited a local bar for a few drinks. When he returned, he found his girl snoring contentedly in bed, limbs sprawled askew. The sound of his stropping a straight razor awakened her.

"What are you gonna do with the razor?" she asked.

Continuing his methodic stropping as he stared at two rolled up towels in the sink, he said, "I'm gonna give myself a shave . . . if these two towels dry soft!"

John had been at the university for more than two years, and his grades had gradually become worse. His father called the dean to find out why.

"Well," the dean replied, "I have good news and I have bad news. Your son is in such poor shape with his school work because he has become a blatant homosexual and does nothing but pursue the boys on the football and basketball teams."

"My God, that's awful!" replied the father. "Tell me quickly, what is the good news?"

The dean replied, "He's been voted Queen of the May."

A bosomy blonde was trying on an extremely low-cut dress. As she studied herself in the mirror, she asked the saleswoman if she thought it was too low-cut.

"Do you have hair on your chest?" the saleswoman asked.

"No!"

"Then," the saleswoman said, "it's too low-cut!"

Once upon a time there was a little sperm. He lived with many thousands of other little sperm, but this little sperm was different. He dreamed endlessly of the glorious day (or night, most likely) when he and his friends would be released to accomplish their great mission in life. The man they inhabited, however, practiced coitus interruptus, and at the moment of orgasm, the small army found itself denied release.

One night, the little sperm told his pals: "Enough of this! The next time he arrives at the point of orgasm, let's make a concentrated rush."

The big moment arrived, but one of the vanguard yelled: "Back up! Back up! He's in the asshole!"

Correct social behavior: In the Catskill resorts couples often share rooms with other couples. Because of this, they frequently indulge in lovemaking under the stars. Should someone happen to step on a recumbent pair, the one stepped on usually says, "Thank you!"

patient at a local hospital was being fed rectally. When a relative of the patient asked his nurse about his progress, she replied, "It would have done your heart good to watch his ass snap at a piece of toast!"

Two hunters were in the woods miles and miles from civilization, when the one had to take a crap. He went into the bushes, but came out screaming, "Joe, Joe, please—While I was in the bushes a snake came and bit the tip of my prick. Please, please, you have to suck out the venom."

To which Joe replied, "Baby, you're going to die!"

A salesman was driving along a lonely stretch of Interstate 95 in a heavy rainstorm, when he spied a hitchhiker. He stopped and picked him up. As they proceeded on their way, the salesman explained that he very rarely picked up a hitchhiker, but the storm was so bad he just had to stop for this man.

The hitchhiker then asked why the salesman did not make it a practice to pick up people on the road. The salesman said, "Well, I used to, until one day when my wife and I picked up a hitchhiker who pulled a gun on us, took our money and clothes, and made my wife get in the back seat and suck him off."

"Well, darling," came the effeminate voice of the hitchhiker, as he pulled his gun, "this just isn't your day."

A young man was extolling the virtues of his beautiful fiancée. One of his closest friends exclaimed, "You can't be serious about marrying Sarah Jane! Why, she's fucked every man in Syracuse."

The bridegroom-to-be thought awhile and then muttered pensively, "Syracuse isn't such a big town."

Two friends, during a pleasurable walk, were engaged in a friendly dispute over the question as to which afforded the greater joy—sexual intercourse or moving the bowels.

As they walked along, a call girl, familiar to both, appeared in their path.

"Let us ask her opinion," said one friend. "She is well experienced in both functions."

The other objected, "She's not the one for an impartial answer. She has slept with men much more frequently than she's been to the john."

Persuasion was necessary, but the amorous swain had finally gotten his girlfriend between the sheets. In due course he made love to her, finally burying his sword in her sheath and beginning to screw away.

"Be careful," she panted. "I think I have a weak heart."

"Don't worry," he said, without missing a stroke. "I'll take it very easy when I get up to the heart!"

A prominent television writer was being ministered to by a talented whore, who was giving him a total body tongue job, more commonly known as a trip around the world. At the same time he was arguing on the telephone with a collaborator over a plot twist on a new television drama on which they were working jointly. The argument got so heated that the whore looked up from her work and complained, "For Christ's sake, argue on your own time."

The writer bellowed into the phone, "We're going to do it my way!" And then he turned to the girl. "And you . . . you keep a civil tongue in my ass!"

An archaeologist, studying a calcified substance he discovered in one of the pharaoh's tombs, somberly presented his findings to the commission. "It is my studied opinion," he said, "that a cat crept into the crypt, crapped, and then crept out again."

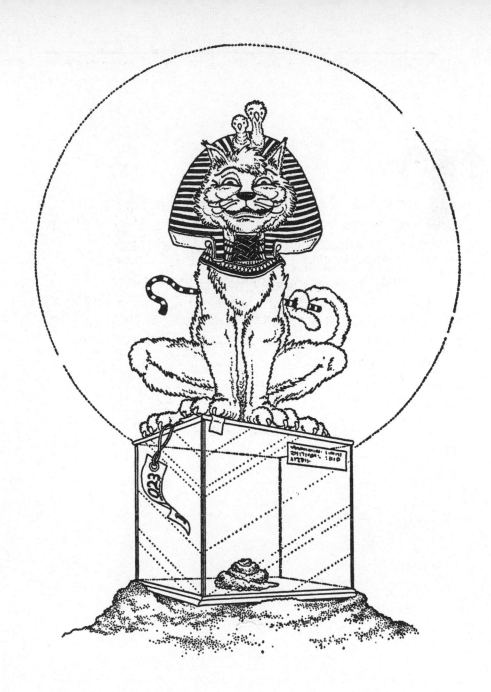

Two ladies of easy virtue were comparing notes at a Las Vegas hotel poolside. "The man I go with gave me two hundred dollars yesterday," said one.

"Gross?" asked the other.

"No, his name was Schwartz."

Diane was a beautiful girl. As she was walking down the lane one hot summer's day, the heat became so unbearable that she decided to go for a swim. She took off her clothes, piled them neatly on the side of the riverbank, and dived in.

A couple of young boys came along and decided to steal her clothes. It grew dark, and Diane just couldn't stay in the water any longer, so she went to the side of the road and decided to hitch a ride home. Along came Mike, riding a bicycle.

He stopped for Diane. "Come," he said. "I'll drive you into town." She jumped on his bicycle.

Mike said nothing, but after ten minutes Diane was so overwhelmed at how cool he was that she said, "Tell me, haven't you noticed that I'm completely naked?"

"Sure," said Mike. "Haven't you noticed that you're riding on a girl's bicycle?"

Sam Cohen was making himself comfortable in Dimples' room in Madame Olga's whorehouse, when the place was suddenly overrun by the police in a surprise raid. As Sam ran down the stairs he zipped up his fly. When he reached the front door he met Irving, a friend and fellow garment manufacturer.

As he headed for his automobile, he yelled, "When the cops disappear, go up to the third floor and throw Dimples a bang. It's paid for!"

A tall, two-hundred-pound Texan, who was a loud braggart, died suddenly of a heart attack. At the funeral services his friends were surprised to note the small size of the coffin.

"That can't be what's left of Big Tom Gallagher," said one of his friends.

"Sure it is!" replied another mourner. "They simply let the bullshit out of him."

B elle Barth talked about a bride who was celebrating the first night of her third honeymoon. Presenting herself as a virgin, she kept crying, "It hurts, it hurts!" while her new husband struggled to twine his feet around the bedpost to keep from falling in.

In desperation, the young bride finally took pen in hand and wrote to Xaviera Hollander:

> I'm married to a sex maniac. My husband never leaves me alone. He makes love to me all night long—while I'm in the shower, while I'm cooking breakfast, while I'm making the beds, and even while I'm trying to clean the house. Can you tell me what to do?
>
> Signed,
> Worn Out
>
> P.S. Please excuse the jerky handwriting.

A young couple were out on a date, attending a concert. The auditorium was pitch dark and, as lovers will, they began to fondle each other. After a while she felt something wet and sticky and realized the boy had come in her hand. She panicked for a moment and then, figuring it was too dark for anyone to see what she was doing, flung the stuff as far in front of her as she could.

It hit the second violinist on the shoulder. He felt something hit him and, trying to get it off, realized what it was.

"Hey," he whispered to the first violinist, "someone just threw me a fuck."

"I'm not surprised," snarled the first violinist. "You've been playing like a cunt all night!"

The third-grade teacher was conducting a class in nutrition and asked the class to name four qualities of mother's milk.

Jimmy said, "I know, teacher. Number one, it's fresh. Number two, it's nutritious. Number three, it's served at just the right temperature. And number four, it comes in such a cute little container."

When queried by his best friend about the joys of his recent marriage, the young bridegroom shook his head disconsolately.

"I'm not sure," he muttered. "When I planned marriage I had dreams of a girl who'd be a lady in the streets, a great cook in the kitchen, and a *nafkeh* [whore] in bed. And what do I have? A *nafkeh* in the streets, a lady in the bedroom, and a great cook . . . never!"

Sam, from the garment center in New York, went to Miami Beach for a winter vacation. While walking down Collins Avenue, he was approached by a luscious blonde, who whispered into his ear, "I'm selling—are you buying?"

Sam said, "Sure, I'm buying."

So they went to a hotel room and made love for the entire night.

A week or so later, when Sam went back to New York, he came down with syphilis. After weeks and weeks of painful treatment, Sam was released by the hospital. As he was walking along Fifth Avenue, the same blonde came over to him and whispered, "I'm selling, mister—are you buying?"

Sam looked her straight in the eye and asked, "So what are you selling now, cancer?"

Adry-goods buyer for a department-store chain was making his annual tour of the mills, searching for fresh merchandise. His trip lasted longer than usual, but he kept in touch with his wife by wiring her nightly: "Still traveling, still buying." After ten days of such wires the wife telegraphed him back: "Come home at once or I'll be selling what you're buying!"

An actor who had drunk too much vodka was faced with the need for instant sobriety. Drinking coffee usually took too long to sober him, but the actor's physician came to the rescue by suggesting a coffee enema as a quick and sure method. The actor agreed and submitted.

As the doctor's nurse was administering the enema he yelled, "Hey! What brand are you using?"

"Maxwell House."

"Forget it," said the actor. "It's the one brand I can't drink."

The stout prostitute disrobed and spread out on the bed awaiting her customer, a newly beached sailor. In his anxiety to relieve his passion he found the wrong opening while poking beneath the rolls of fat.

"You're in the wrong hole!" she screamed.

"Any port in a storm," said the sailor, pressing on.

Belle Barth told the story of the sweet young thing who was taken to a fancy East Side restaurant in New York by her elderly employer. After a few cocktails, the young lady ordered a pâté de foie gras, an endive salad, chateaubriand, and dessert and coffee. She did not omit a fine wine.

The old gentleman stared quizzically at her: "Your mother feeds you this way?" he asked.

"No," replied the sweet young thing, "but my mother's not looking to fuck me, either!"

The bright young man working in the produce section of a large supermarket in Detroit was approached by a customer.

"I want half a head of lettuce," the man said.

"Sir, we can't sell half a head of lettuce," the young clerk explained.

The man persisted and the young man agreed to check with the store's manager.

He found the manager and said, "Mr. Peterson, I've got some nut in the produce department who wants to buy half a head of lettuce." Just as he finished his statement he saw that the customer had followed him and was standing next to him. "And this gentleman," he said hastily, "wants to buy the other half."

"Sell it," the manager said.

Later, the manager took the youth aside. "That was quick thinking," he said. "We need bright young men like you, and I'm going to keep my eyes open on your behalf."

"Thanks, Mr. Peterson," the young man said.

Two weeks later he was summoned by the manager.

"Well, my lad, I told you I'd watch out for you, and indeed I have. I've recommended you for an assistant manager's job in our new store in Montreal—"

"Montreal!" the young man exclaimed. "Why,

nothing comes from there except hookers and hockey players!"

Peterson said, "Listen, young fellow, my wife comes from there!"

Without missing a beat, the young man replied, "No kidding! What position does she play?"

Giovanni lived in Palermo, Italy. One day he arrived from work early, to find his wife in bed with Pietro, the butcher.

The wife screamed; Pietro screamed.

Meanwhile, Giovanni ran to the closet, pulled out a pistol, and faced his wife.

He put the barrel of the pistol to his forehead and smirked at her: "Don't feel sorry for me, you bitch. You're gonna be next!"

There was a hurried inspection call at the marine base in Camp Lagoon. Most of the marines were caught in bed naked and had no time to dress, so they lined up outside the barracks shivering and nude. As the marine sergeant went down the line, he saw one of the recruits with an impressive hardon. He walked up to it and gave it a vicious swat with his club. Expecting the recruit to be doubed over in pain, the sergeant was amazed that he stood there with a big smile on his face.

He exclaimed to the recruit, "My God, I can't believe it. I just swatted your penis, and you stand there and smile back at me."

The recruit answered, "I'm smiling because the cock belongs to the man behind me "

Two business partners, both married, were taking turns having intercourse with their attractive secretary. As a result of such frequent fucking, the young lady became pregnant with twins.

One partner, congratulating the other, said, "Susie had twins. Unfortunately, mine died!"

George took his girlfriend to bed for the first time. He was working away very hard, but she was not responding at all. Finally, in exasperation, he asked her, "What's the matter?"

She said: "It's your organ. I don't think it's big enough."

To which George replied, "Well, I didn't think I'd be playing in a cathedral!"

Jones, returning from a business trip, was surprised to find his wife in bed with a strange man. The stranger, nude and obviously well satisfied, was sprawled over the bed.

"Why, you rotten bastard!" the husband exploded.

"Wait, darling," said Mrs. Jones. "You know that fur coat I got last winter? This man gave it to me. Remember the diamond necklace you like so much? This man gave it to me. And remember when you couldn't afford a second car and I got a Toyota? This man gave it to me."

"For heaven's sake, it's drafty here!" shouted the husband "Cover him so he doesn't catch cold!"

A wealthy Jewish lawyer was unhappy over the romantic pursuits of his junior-college son. He told his closest friend, "My son's a homosexual." But then he added, "The situation could be worse, though. He's in love with a doctor."

Jim and Tom were sitting in a saloon hoisting a few drinks.

Jim remarked: "My wife is the ugliest woman who was ever born."

"She can't be," replied Tom. "My wife is the ugliest woman you've ever seen."

They argued for about fifteen minutes, and Jim finally said, "Look, Tom—I'll bet you $100 that my wife is the ugliest woman you've ever come across." He removed a wallet from his pocket and took out her picture.

"Okay," Tom conceded. "She is ugly. Now come home with me and I'll show you my wife."

They walked to Tom's house, and Tom walked directly to his den. He rolled up the rug on the floor. Under the rug was a trap door. He lifted up the trap door and yelled into the darkness below, "Come on up, darling."

The wife replied, "All right, dear, I'm coming, but do you want me to put the bag over my head?"

"Not this time," Joe said. "I don't want to fuck you, honey. I just want to show you off."

Airline hostess: "Would you like some of our TWA coffee?"

Passenger: "No, thank you, but I'd love some of your TWA tea."

A young man, anxious for some sexual exercise, picked up a hot little number in Central Park, not realizing that she was a nymphomaniac. He took her to a hotel. After six times, she was screaming for more. After the seventh, exhausted, he slipped out of the room on the pretense of buying cigarettes. He stopped in the men's room, unzipped his fly, and couldn't find anything.

In a panic he reached inside his shorts. It was still there, but tiny and all drawn up. In a soothing voice he whispered, "It's all right. You can come out now. She's not here!"

The recruits for the college football team were lined up to take their first physical before the new coach and, of course, were stripped naked. Charlie, the candidate for the tight end job, stepped before the coach, who was amazed to see that Charlie's cock was about sixteen inches long but only half an inch thick.

The coach exclaimed, "Charlie what the hell happened to you?"

Charlie explained, "Listen, I was nineteen years old before I found out you weren't supposed to roll it between your hands."

Stan did a hitch in the navy, which kept him away for eighteen months, during which his beautiful young wife sat at home awaiting his return.

On the first day of his leave she spied him entering their apartment house and quickly ran to the bedroom, throwing off all her clothes. She sat there breathlessly until she heard Stan's heavy knocking at the door.

"Darling," she yelled as she ran to fling it open, "I know why you're knocking."

"Yes," he gasped, "but do you know what I'm knocking with?"

The elderly couple, celebrating their golden anniversary, had a night on the town. After they prepared for bed the husband reached across the felt for his wife's hand.

"Not tonight, dear," she said, withdrawing her hand. "I'm too tired."

A concerned patient visited his physician and asked him if masturbation was harmful.

"No," the doctor said. "Not if you don't do it too often."

"How about three times a day?"

"That seems a little excessive. Why don't you get yourself a girl?"

"I've got a girl," the patient said.

"I mean a girl you can live with and sleep with."

"I've got one like that."

"Then why in heaven's name do you masturbate three times a day?"

"Oh," said the patient disgustedly, "she doesn't like it during mealtimes."

A bishop in a small Midwestern town bought two parrots and taught them to say the rosary. He even had two sets of tiny rosary beads made for them.

After months of exhaustive training, the parrots were able to recite the rosary and use the beads at the same time. The bishop was so pleased that he decided to teach another parrot the rosary. He went to the pet store and bought a female parrot, which he brought home and put into the cage with the other two.

As he did this, one parrot turned to the other and said, "Throw away your beads, George—our prayers have been answered!"

This is the true story of Cinderella, who was the most promiscuous bitch in the entire kingdom. She never said no. She never even said maybe. One day, the fairy godmother appeared and said, "Cinderella, you just have to stop screwing everybody who approaches you. You'll never be able to marry the prince unless you do."

Cinderella promised and tried her damnedest, but only a week after her talk with the fairy godmother she was caught in bed with the chimney sweep and his two assistants. The fairy godmother became so enraged that she changed Cinderella's pussy into a pumpkin!

Two weeks later, the fairy godmother, paying another visit to see how Cinderella was doing, caught her singing and dancing and smiling—a very happy girl. "Why are you smiling?" asked the fairy godmother.

"Because I've just met Peter Peter!" was the reply.

The customer in a bordello was dismayed to see the unshaven armpits of the hooker as she undressed.

"So much wool, so much wool!" he muttered.

As she slipped off her panties, he noticed another prodigious growth.

"So much wool, so much wool!" he exclaimed again.

The girl retorted, "Look, mister, did you come here to get laid or to knit?"

Jack was enthusiastic over the new girl he had found at the neighborhood massage parlor. "You like three-way broads," he told his friend. "Well, this one knows four ways."

"What's the fourth way?" asked his friend.

"She lets you go down on her."

The dictionaries have different definitions, but we all know that an optimist says the glass is half-full while the pessimist sees it as half-empty. Others know that an optimist is a girl who doesn't take a pessimist with her on a cruise.

Stanley was taking his very first airplane ride and had been so nervous that he had been plagued by constipation for a full week before the flight.

Finally flight day came, and after takeoff he felt so much better that he decided to move to the back of the plane and visit one of the lavatories.

While Stanley was having a hard time relieving himself, he heard the door to the adjacent lavatory open and close. He listened while a gentleman relieved himself loudly.

Stanley sighed through the thin partition: "I can tell that you were constipated too, but it's great to hear that you've been lucky."

To which the man replied: "It's a big relief, and it will be even better when I get my pants down!"

Girl in movie house: "The man next to me is masturbating!"

Girlfriend: "Ignore him."

"I can't; he's using my hand!"

Farmer Brown had been screwing one of his pigs for four years, when he was suddenly hit by pangs of conscience. It tortured him so much that he decided to tell the priest about it in confession.

The priest was shocked and could only say to Farmer Brown, "Well, tell me, was the pig a male or a female?"

"A female, of course," said Farmer Brown. "What do you think I am—some sort of a queer?"

Sam had been a soldier at war for more than three years, during which he had been in many battles and won many decorations. He was finally discharged from service and returned home to a wife and son whom he hadn't seen in almost four years.

As he was walking up the path to his house, his young son spotted him and yelled, "Mommy, Mommy, here comes Daddy, and he's got a purple heart on!" to which the mother replied, "I don't give a damn what color it is! Let him in, and you go play at the Joneses' for a couple of hours."

How do porcupines make love? V-e-r-y carefully!

The young farmer who had just taken a bride was concerned over his ability to perform on his nuptial night. When it came bedtime he attempted to exercise his conjugal duty, to no avail.

The next day he visited his local doctor and explained the problem. "The opening one customarily expects to find in a woman is missing," he said.

The doctor gave the matter much consideration and concluded that the bride must spend time with him. The farmer agreed, and the young bride repaired to the doctor's house

The next day the anxious husband inquired about results.

"Excellent results," said the doctor. "I labored and labored for hours with your wife. For a while I thought it was hopeless, but I am pleased to tell you that her love canal is now rosy and open and as slick as oil. Enjoy yourself, and my fee will be moderate."

The grateful farmer paid his bill.

Morris left for a two-day business trip to Chicago. He was only a few blocks from his house, when he realized that he had left the airplane tickets on his bureau top. He returned and quietly entered the house. His wife, in her skimpiest negligee, was standing at the sink washing the breakfast dishes.

She looked so inviting that he tiptoed up behind her, reached out, and squeezed her left tit.

"Leave only one quart of milk," she said. "Morris won't be here for breakfast tomorrow."

General Custer's troops had just come from a tremendous battle with the Indians in which the Indians were badly defeated. After the troops had left to return to the fort, the Indian chief called his tribe together and said, "I must report on the battle. There is good news and there is bad news. The bad news is that we were soundly trounced by the American troopers. They burned down our camp, raped our women, and took our food supplies. We'll have nothing to eat throughout this cold winter except buffalo turds."

The chief's son piped up: "If that's the bad news, what's the good news?"

The chief said, "There are plenty of buffalo out here."

The new husband, a Cockney stagehand, had a most satisfactory nuptial night with his young bride. Forgetting his marital state he quickly dressed himself, threw several half-crowns on the bureau, and headed for the door. On the way out he recalled his new status and returned to his bride. There he found her biting on the coins in an experienced manner.

Girls who use their heads can stop the population explosion.

What were the first words Eve used when she beheld Adam?

"Don't stick that thing in me!"

Joe was selling chance books for the Sacramental Softball and Social Society. During his first day's work, he came upon Mrs. Skettington, an old lady who lived on his block. He knocked on her door and said, "Mrs. Skettington, would you please buy some chances for the Sacramental Softball and Social Society?"

Mrs. Skettington answered, "I'm hard of hearing. What is that you're selling?"

"I'm selling chances for the Sacramental Softball and Social Society."

"What's that?" she said.

In disgust, Joe turned his back and walked away, muttering, "Fuck you, Mrs. Skettington," under his breath.

To which Mrs. Skettington answered, "Well, fuck the Sacramental Softball and Social Society!"

**S**he snuggled up to him and murmured, "I'm yours for the asking. . . . I'm asking fifty dollars."

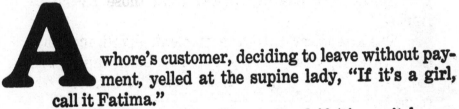**A** whore's customer, deciding to leave without payment, yelled at the supine lady, "If it's a girl, call it Fatima."

"Fine," said the whore, "and if it's an itch, you call it eczema!"

A stately-looking matron was walking through the Bronx Zoo, studying the animals. When she passed the porcupine enclosure she beckoned to a nearby attendant.

"Young man," she began, "do the North American porcupines have sharper pricks than those raised in Africa?"

The attendant thought a moment. "Well, ma'am," he answered, "the African porcupine's quills are sharper . . . but I think their pricks are about the same."

D ouglas was a bit of a nut who enjoyed making obscene phone calls. His biggest pleasure, however, was to make such calls to kindergarten teachers.

He'd find a lonely telephone booth, dial the number of some teacher, and exclaim, "Is this Mrs. Jones, the kindergarten teacher at P.S. 22?

"It is? Well, wee-wee, poo-poo, ca-ca!"

A kindly young woman saw a little boy standing on a street curb attempting to relieve himself. Giving in to her maternal instincts, the woman helped the lad release his organ from his pants. She evinced considerable surprise when the organ proved to be a man-sized tool, growing in her hand as the lad sighed with relief. "How old are you, little man?" she asked.

"Thirty-three, ma'am," answered the pint-sized jockey.

P apa," said the farmer's son, "you were a sheepherder in your younger days; perhaps you can tell me where virgin wool comes from."

"Virgin wool, my son, comes from the sheep the herders couldn't catch."

STILL MORE OF

The World's Best Dirty Jokes

Mr. "J"

Foreword

No gentleman has ever heard a story before.
ANON.

This is the third and final volume of Mr. "J" 's collections of the world's best dirty jokes. Reader reaction to the first two collections, *The World's Best Dirty Jokes* and *More of the World's Best Dirty Jokes,* was so positive that the author again searched his vast storehouse of material for jokes and stories worthy of inclusion.

Some of the jokes and stories are new; some you may have read (or heard) in different versions. Most of them might merit being X-rated. But we believe you and your friends can pick up this book and enjoy hours of smiles, chuckles and plain old belly laughs.

"Laughter is the most inexpensive and most effective wonder drug Laughter is a universal medicine "
BERTRAND RUSSELL

Three coeds were talking about a guy each had dated during the past few weeks.

The first said, "He thinks he's pretty sophisticated, so I decided to teach him a lesson. When I went to his room I found his condoms lying on the table. I stuffed them into one of his socks so he couldn't find them and, boy, did that cramp his style."

The second girl said, "I thought that a sock was a peculiar place to keep rubbers. But I really took care of him. Since it was my period, I didn't worry about getting laid, but I did take the rubbers and punctured each one and put them back in the drawer where he could find them."

The third coed fainted.

An Englishman, a Pole and a Puerto Rican were standing atop the Empire State building, bemoaning their respective fates. Disgusted with their lives the three formed a suicide pact.

The Briton jumped first, sailing neatly to his doom . . . the Pole got lost on the way down . . . and the Puerto Rican stopped every few floors to scribble "Fuck you!" on the walls.

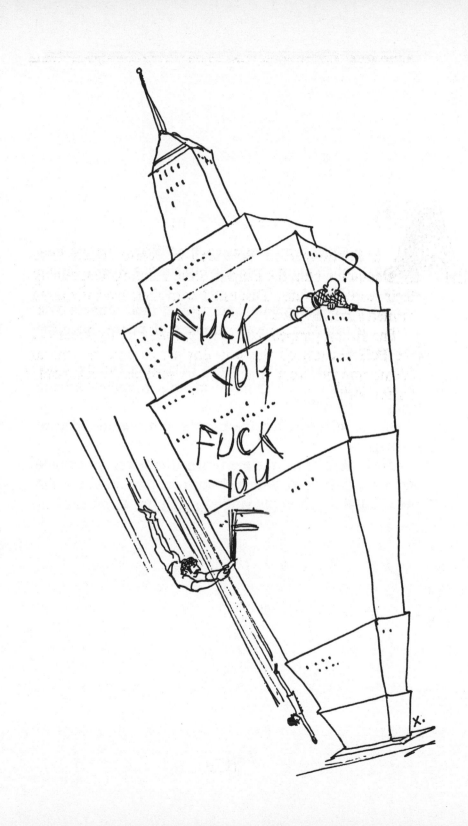

Two couples who had been great friends since they had gotten married decided to share a Rocky Mountain vacation.

They pitched two tents and cooked their dinners over a roaring campfire. Ample supplies of booze made the food tastier.

When it came bedtime, one of the men asked the other three: "What do you think of all this switching around that's going on?"

The question excited the others, and they decided to experiment.

After a few hours, the man turned to his new bedmate and said, "I haven't had such a great time in years. Do you think the girls are having as much fun as we are?"

An inexperienced young man, prior to his wedding, asked his father how to conduct himself.

"Well," said the father, "you take the thing you used to play with when you were a teenager and put it where your wife wee-wees."

So the young man took his baseball and threw it in the toilet.

An airplane passenger, being served drinks by the stewardess, exclaimed: "Hey, here's something new ... an ice cube with a hole in it!"

"What's new about that?" answered the man sitting alongside. "I married one."

A traveling salesman, completing a trip earlier than anticipated, sent his wife a telegram: "Returning home Friday."

Arriving home, he found his wife in bed with another man. Being a person of non-violence, he complained to his father-in-law, who said, "I'm sure there must be an explanation."

The next day the father-in-law was all smiles. "I knew there was an explanation. She didn't get your telegram."

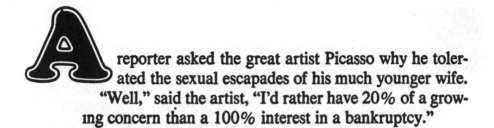

reporter asked the great artist Picasso why he tolerated the sexual escapades of his much younger wife. "Well," said the artist, "I'd rather have 20% of a growing concern than a 100% interest in a bankruptcy."

What do they call a Chinese voyeur?
A Peiping Tom.

ilas and Sally were in the cornfield behind the barn, happily fucking away.

It had rained a lot that day and the earth was muddy. The bare-assed couple were slipping around a good deal.

Silas became concerned. "Say, honey," he asked, "is my cock in you or is it in the mud?"

Sally felt down and said, "Why, honey, it's in the mud."

"Well, put it back in you," Silas sighed.

Things seemed to be going okay, but Silas still had his doubts.

"Say, honey, is it in you or in the mud?"

"Why, Silas, it's in me," Sally cooed happily.

"Well, put it back in the mud."

While dancing at Roseland, a man assayed small talk with his partner. "Honey, do you know the minuet?" "Hell, no," she replied, "I don't even know the men I've laid."

The aged patient toddered into the doctor's office with a serious complaint.

"Doc, you've got to do something to lower my sex drive."

"Come on now, Mr. Peters," the dostor said, "your sex drive's all in your head."

"That's what I mean; you've got to lower it a little."

Not in Webster's Dictionary: Definition of a gynecologist as a spreader of old wives' tales.

LITTLE BOY: "Mama, where do babies come from?"
MAMA: "From the stork, of course."
LITTLE BOY: "But, Mama, who fucks the stork?"

How do you make Manischewitz wine?
Squeeze his balls!

F rank and Ronald—a married-without-benefit-of-clergy homosexual couple—had been spending a quiet evening at home.

"Hey, Ronald," Frank called out, "has the paper boy come yet?"

"Not yet, but he's getting a glassy look in his eyes."

Recent Graffiti in the Men's Washrooms

The crying crabs . . . it crawls up your legs and bawls.

Stand up close to the urinal . . . the next guy may be barefoot.

If you sprinkle when you tinkle . . . be a sweetie and wipe the seatie.

Hey, Bud, stand up closer . . . you've got a pistol in your hand, not a Winchester.

Chuck was always shy with girls.

One evening, he got his best friend, Bob, to go with him to a singles bar. Bob, being very experienced, was supposed to help Chuck in his quest for female companionship, and sexual companionship.

One sweet young thing in the room noticed Chuck, thought he was cute, and decided to make contact with him. Since she was a little shy, she could not just go up to him, but had to use gestures.

"Bob," Chuck said. "That girl over there is giving me the eye. What should I do?"

"Give her the eye back," replied Bob.

So Chuck, as best as he could, gave her the eye.

A few moments passed.

"Bob," said Chuck, now getting rather excited. "She's smiling at me. What do I do?"

"Smile back," was the reply.

So Chuck, trying to appear cool and calm, smiled back

A few more moments passed.

"Bob! ! !" exclaimed Chuck. "My God. She bent over and showed me her tits. Now what do I do?"

"Show her your nuts," Bob calmly replied.

So Chuck turned toward the girl, stuck his thumbs in his ears, and waving his fingers stuck out his tongue, and wiggling it, exclaimed, "Bluble, bluble, bluble!"

Two soldiers were canvassing the streets in a new town when a girl popped out of a doorway and cried: "Hey, fellows, come on in and I'll give you something you've never had before."

One soldier grabbed the other's arm and said, "Let's get the hell out of here. She's got leprosy."

Two buddies at the bar, drinking away, were comparing the sexual behavior of their spouses.

"Hey," one asked, "does your wife close her eyes when you're pumping away on her?"

"She sure does," replied the other. "She just can't stand to watch me having a good time."

Millie was complaining to Janis that her latest lover only wants to "eat it."

Janis said, "You're a lucky girl, but if you want to discourage him, why not rub garlic in your pussy?"

"I tried that," said Millie, "but the next night he came to bed with some lettuce and olive oil."

The woman had been away for two days visiting a sick friend in another city. When she returned, her little boy greeted her by saying, "Mommy, guess what! Yesterday I was playing in the closet in your bedroom and Daddy came into the room with the lady next door and they got undressed and got into your bed and then Daddy got on top of her————"

Sonny's mother held up her hand. "Not another word. Wait till your father comes home and then I want you to tell him exactly what you've just told me."

The father came home. As he walked into the house, his wife said, "I'm leaving you. I'm packing now and I'm leaving you."

"But why————" asked the startled father.

"Go ahead, Sonny. Tell Daddy just what you told me."

"Well," Sonny said, "I was playing in your bedroom closet and Daddy came upstairs with the lady next door and they got undressed and got into bed and Daddy got on top of her and then they did just what you did with Uncle John when Daddy was away last summer."

A guy had his male cat "fixed" because he was a menace to the neighborhood, sneaking out at night and impregnating all the neighbors' female cats.

The tom still sneaks out at night . . but now he acts as a consultant.

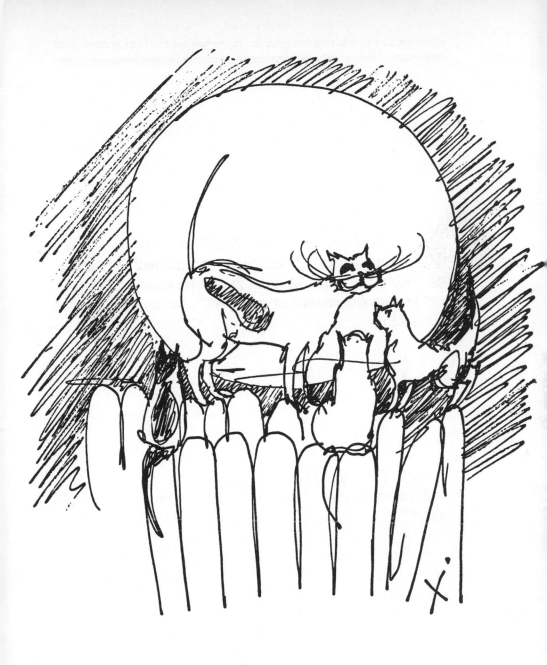

verheard at a cocktail party: A husband was asking his wife, "Tell me, dear, before we married, did you say you were oversexed or over sex?"

FIRST DRUNK: "My wife is an angel."
SECOND DRUNK: "You're lucky . . . my wife is still alive!"

A disappointed father, expecting a son, complained to the doctor that he was anticipating a baby with a penis.

"Yes," said the doctor, "but just imagine that in about eighteen years, she'll have a beautiful place to put one in."

There was an old man from Nantucket
Whose cock was so long
He could suck it.
He said, with a grin,
As he wiped off his chin:
If my ear was a cunt,
I could fuck it!

Two men sitting side by side were having their respective scalps tonsured. The first barber asked his client if he'd like some French toilet water on his hair.

"Oh, no," the man said. "My wife would think I'd been in a French whorehouse."

The second barber asked the same question of his client, who said, "Why, sure, my wife has never been in a French whorehouse."

n unfortunate young man was thrown out of the Boy Scouts for eating Brownies.

ittle William went to his father and said, "Daddy, where did I come from?"

The father started to stutter and stammer, but he realized that he had to tell his son the facts of life.

"Sit down, Willie," he said.

At great length, he described the whole business of creation, beginning with the birds and the bees. Then he went into the most graphic descriptions of human intercourse.

He concluded at last, feeling limp and drained. He took a kerchief and wiped the perspiration from his brow. "Okay, Willie, do you understand now?"

Willie scratched his head. "Not really, Dad. Henry says he came from New Jersey but you haven't told me where I come from."

A man and his attractive companion were enjoying a cocktail party where one of the other female guests was expounding her philosophy. "I guess I'm just an animal," she was saying, "all I want to do is sleep and make love." The man's companion agreed, "I sleep and make love too."

"Yes," the man said, "but do you do both at the same time!"

Pole was suffering from constipation, so his doctor prescribed suppositories.

A week later the Pole complained to the doctor that they didn't produce the desired results.

"Have you been taking them regularly?" the doctor asked.

"What do you think I've been doing," the Pole said, "shoving them up my ass?"

A pigeon invited his friends to the top of the World Trade Center in New York. As he flew past the observation deck he answered a call of nature. The other pigeons watched as his droppings floated gracefully to the street.

"See, fellows," the pigeon said, "a little shit goes a long way in this town."

The little Jewish man was sitting on a bench at Atlantic City saying, "They're wonderful! They're marvelous! They're magnificent!"

A policeman sauntered over to him. "What are you talking about, me lad?"

The man on the bench replied: "I've just been reading history. That Israeli army—look how they beat those Arabs."

The cop said, "Fuck the Israeli army!"

The man on the bench looked a little aghast. "Well, take the late Prime Minister, Golda Meir. Didn't she run things well? What a woman she was!"

The cop said, "Fuck Golda Meir!"

The man on the bench thought for a minute and then said, "Well, take the way those immigrants have taken a barren desert and built it—"

The cop said, "Fuck those immigrants and their barren desert!"

The little man stared up at the cop. "Excuse me, officer. What nationality are you?"

"What do you think I am? I'm Irish, of course."

And the man on the bench said, "Fuck Ella Fitzgerald!"

A man went to a plastic surgeon to get work done on his penis.

The doctor, curious, asked what had happened to it.

"Well," the patient said, "I live in a trailer camp. A gorgeous buxom creature lives in the trailer next to mine. I used to peek into her trailer and I saw that she had a habit. Each afternoon she'd take a frankfurter from her refrigerator and put it in a hole on her trailer floor. Then she'd sit on it and have a ball.

"She nearly drove me crazy. So I got a bright idea. One day I got under her trailer and when she slid the frankfurter into the hole, I slid it out and slipped my cock up through the hole.

"She sat down on it and everything was going just great until there was a knock at the door."

"And then?" said the doctor.

"Aw hell," the patient explained. "That's when she tried to kick it under the stove."

A gay guy used to hang out in the neighborhood drugstore, where the gang always greeted him by saying, "Hello, cunt."

The homosexual never reacted. One day, however, after the usual "Hello, cunt" greeting, the gay said vehemently: "Don't you call me that!"

"Why not?" the head of the gang wanted to know.

"Because," he lisped, "the other day I saw one."

Little Gwen opened the back door to the kitchen where her mother was cooking dinner.

"Mom," she asked, "can a nine-year-old girl become pregnant?"

"Of course not," her mother said.

Gwen turned around. "Okay, fellows," she called, "let's continue playing the game."

Doreen was in bed, anxiously waiting for her date to take off his pants. When he did and she saw the size of his organ, she jumped out of bed and ran to the desk drawer.

"What the hell are you doing?" he cried.

"I'm getting a crayon," she said. "You've got to draw the line somewhere."

An armless man walked into John's Bar and ordered a beer. When served, he asked the bartender to help him drink it by holding the glass. This was done cheerfully and then repeated twice. After the third beer, the customer asked the location of the men's room. The bartender pointed to the rear of the bar but intoned sternly, "You go there, alone."

Four men had played golf together for two years. At the conclusion of the games, three of the men always showered together and then had a few drinks at the bar. The fourth man would hurry home.

One day one of the trio asked the fourth man, "Listen, how come you never stick around?"

The fourth man was uncomfortable. "All right, I'll tell you. I don't stay because I don't want to shower with you. I'm embarrassed because my penis is very small."

The other man asked, "Does it work?"

"Sure, it works very well."

"Well how would you like to trade it for one that looks good in the shower?"

The recently married bride was perplexed when her husband announced that he had found a new position.

"What's that, honey?"

"We lie back to back."

"But, what kind of position is that?"

"You'll see. Another couple is joining us."

My friend was telling a pal that he had a dream that he was alone in a boat with Dolly Parton. His pal asked, "Really, how did you make out?" My friend said, "Great, I caught a twelve-pound bass."

hat is the meaning of the word indecent? When it's firm and long and thrust to the hilt, then it's indecent.

 divorcee took an office job and said. "I hope I'll find sexual harassment on the job."

Two kids were having the standard argument about whose father could beat up whose father.

One boy said, "My father is better than your father."

The other kid said, "Well, my mother is better than your mother."

The first boy paused, "I guess you're right. My father says the same thing."

An old gentleman slowly approached the local brothel and pressed the doorbell.

The madam opened the door, looked at the old fellow with a critical eye and then asked: "What can we do for you, sir?"

"I need a girl," the senior citizen said.

"For you, the charge is a hundred dollars."

"You're putting me on," he exclaimed.

"That will be an extra ten dollars," said the madam.

An important executive was telling friends at his country club about some of his experiences. "So I bought this yacht that could carry fifty people and I took it out for a maiden voyage and it hit a reef and sunk.

"Then I bought an airplane and on the first flight it hit another plane on the field and it burned up.

"Then I married this beautiful blonde and no sooner did I get home than I found her fooling around with the chauffeur and I had to divorce her."

"So what's the moral?" one of the others asked.

"Clear as a bell," said the old man. "If it swims, flies or fucks, lease it, don't buy it."

Two elderly priests and a young novitiate wanted to buy train tickets to Pittsburgh at a railway station. The young girl selling tickets was pretty and endowed with a large and shapely set of breasts, set off by a V-neck that displayed her mammaries to great advantage every time she bent forward.

The young novitiate approached the ticket booth and said, "Miss, please give me three tickets to Tittsville."

"How dare you?" remonstrated the ticket seller.

The first priest said, "Let me handle this. Miss," he stammered, "three pickets to Tittsburgh, please, and give me the change in nipples and dimes."

The second priest, the eldest of the trio, tried to placate the angry young woman.

"Three tickets to Pittsburgh, please, and you should dress more decorously, young woman, or Saint Finger is going to point his peter at you!"

omeone left the zebra's cage open in the middle of the night and he escaped and ran away to a local farm.

Early the next morning, he approached an old hen, saying, "What do you do around here?"

The hen replied, "I lay eggs for the farmer's breakfast."

The zebra then walked over to the cow, asking, "What do you do?"

The cow replied, "I give milk for the farmer's breakfast."

The zebra then spied an enormous bull and asked the same question.

The bull looked at the zebra with a quizzical smile and said: "Listen, you queer ass, take off those faggy pajamas and I'll show you what I do around here."

It was the first Christmas and the first of the Three Wise Men slowly approached the barn and gingerly crossed over the threshold—into a big juicy pile of horse shit.

Looking down at his gold slippers, he let out a shriek— "Je-sus Christ!"

The woman at the manger turned to her companion and said, "Joseph, that's a better name for the kid than Irving."

The henpecked husband was asked why he couldn't bear to sit through porno movies.

"I can't stand one guy enjoying himself more in ten minutes than I have in the last twenty years."

Not in Mother Goose Rhymes

Y stands for Yanker,
The self-driving chap.
He greases his pole and
Provokes his own sap.

Absolved of the need of
A quarrelsome wife,
He humps himself nightly
And lives a great life.

Three women were bragging about what great husbands they married.

The first said, "My husband is fantastic. He bought me two mink coats and an ermine wrap."

The second said, "My husband bought me two sailboats and also a yacht that twelve people can live on."

"My husband is poor," said the third woman, "but you can have your rich husbands with their fur coats and their yachts. My husband is very special. He has a penis so long that thirteen birds can stand on it side by side."

There was a long silence. The first woman said, "Listen, I was lying to you. My husband didn't get me all those fancy coats. He bought me one small cloth coat at Alexanders and I'm very happy with it."

The second woman said, "Well, since we're telling the truth, you might as well know I didn't get two sailboats and a fancy yacht. All I got was a rowboat ride in Central Park."

Both women turned and stared at the third.

"Okay, okay!" she said. "So I'll tell the truth too. The business about the thirteen birds who can stand side by side on my husband's penis is not true. The thirteenth bird can only stand on one leg."

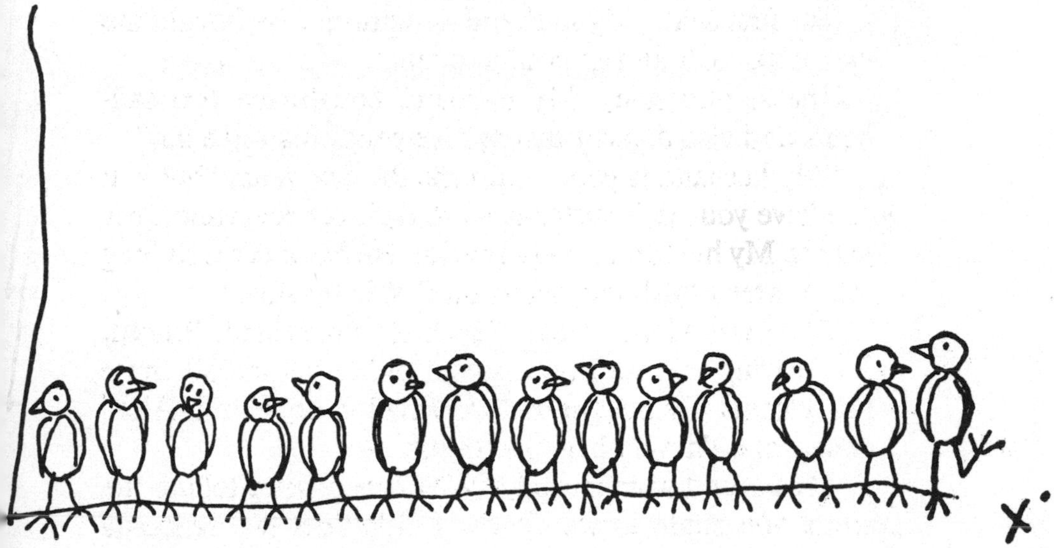

The tough character was mumbling to his friend, "My girl, Mary, is going to die of syphilis."

"No," the friend said, "people don't die of syphilis anymore."

"They do when they give it to me!" was the rejoinder.

A businessman who had his life savings wiped out in the market came home and told his wife, "Honey, I'm absolutely busted, penniless. We have to start all over again."

The wife shuddered, saying, "I can't change my way of life; I'd rather be dead." And with that she leaped out of the open window.

The newly widowed husband smiled: "Thank you, Paine, Webber . . ."

A fellow has a girlfriend whose bedroom is done entirely in mirrors: walls, ceiling, the whole bit. When he calls on her he brings along a bottle of Ajax Window Cleaner.

CENSORED MOTHER GOOSE

I

Charley loves good cake and ale;
Charley loves good candy;
Charley loves to——— the girls—
When they are clean and handy.

II

See-saw, Margaret Daw,
Jenny shall have a new master;
She shall have but a penny a day
Because she can't——— any faster.

Sam was very worried. His teenage daughter was hitch-hiking home from Miami to Minneapolis by herself. She was seventeen but was built like she was twenty-five. When she arrived home unscathed her father was curious as to how she avoided rape, if not worse.

"I simply told all the men who picked me up that I was going to the clinic in Minneapolis because it's the number one establishment in the country for curing V.D." she replied sweetly.

Through the first four holes in the golf course, Jim was very quiet. Finally, on the fifth tee, John asked, "What the hell's the matter, Jim? You're so silent."

"It's my wife, Ann," John replied. "Ever since she's been working overtime at the phone company, she's cut our sex down to twice a week."

"You're lucky," replied John. "She's cut me off completely."

So this old man went to his doctor.
"I've got toilet problems," he complained.
"Well, let's see. How is your urination?"
"Every morning at seven o'clock like a baby."
"Good. How about your bowel movement?"
"Eight o'clock each morning like clockwork."
"So what's the problem?" the doctor asked.
"I don't wake up until nine!"

There once was a girl from Jahore
Who'd lie on a rug on the floor.
In a manner uncanny, she'd wiggle her fanny
And drain your balls dry to the core.

There once was a lady from France
Who took a long train ride by chance.
The engineer fucked her before the conductor
While the fireman came in his pants.

A young man in love with a girl he wanted to fuck was so ashamed of his small penis that he was afraid of bringing up the question, or of letting her see him naked.

One dark night he drove her around in his car and parked in a dark lane. As they kissed he surreptitiously opened his fly and put his weapon in her hand.

"Thanks," she said. "But you know I don't smoke."

A patient, suffering from an impacted wisdom tooth, went to his dentist.

"That tooth has got to be pulled immediately," the dentist said as he reached for a wicked-looking set of forceps.

The patient reached out and got a tight grip on the dentist's balls. "We're not going to hurt each other, are we, doctor?"

The census taker asked a girl to give her occupation.
"Whore," she answered.
"I can't list it that way, Miss."
"Okay, put down prostitute."
"I can't list it that way either."
"How about chicken raiser?"
"Chicken raiser?" he asked in puzzlement.
"Sure, last year I raised nine hundred cocks."

harlie was telling his tale of woe to his boss. He said, "I was so drunk last night that I don't know how I got home. Not realizing it was my bed I slept in when I awoke, I handed the woman next to me a $20 bill."

"Is that what's making you sad?"

"No," said Charlie. "It was my wife I gave the $20 to, but she gave me $10 change."

Maw told her son Clem to check out the family outdoor one-holer.

"Tain't nothin' wrong with it, Maw," Clem insisted. But she took him out to the outhouse and made him stick his head down inside the hole.

"Maw," he called from the depths, "my beard's stuck!"

"Aggravatin', ain't it?" said Maw.

MORE CENSORED MOTHER GOOSE

I

Bobby Shafto's gone to sea;
Silver buckles on his knee;
When he comes back he'll——— me.
Pretty Bobby Shafto.

II

A diller, a dollar.
A two o'clock scholar.
What makes you——— so soon?
You used to———at two o'clock,
But now you——— at noon.

A long-married wife told her husband that he should experiment with eating her pussy, as she had heard it was a thrilling experience. The husband, who had never heard of such a thing, went manfully to the task. The taste wasn't bad but the smell was overpowering. Suddenly the wife orgasmed and, simultaneously, emitted a tremendous fart.

"Thank God," sighed the husband, "for a breath of fresh air!"

novice nun was permitted to say only two words per year in the cloister of her particular order. Each year she did this in response to a question posed by the Mother Superior.

The first year the Mother Superior asked her, "How do you like it here, Sister?"

"Bad food," was the novice's reply.

At the end of the second year the Mother Superior asked her, "How do you like it here, Sister?"

"Poor company," was the terse reply.

At the end of the third year, the Mother Superior again asked her favorite question, but this time the novice nun replied: "I quit."

"I'm not surprised," said the Mother Superior. "You have been here three years now, Sister, and all you've done is bitch, bitch, bitch!"

An American traveling in the United Kingdom was riding in a British train compartment with an Englishman and an elderly English lady with her pet Pekinese.

They had traveled only a short distance when the dog threw up over the American's trousers.

Instead of apologizing, the Englishwoman fondled her dog and comforted it saying, "Poor itsy-bitsy doggie has a little tummy ache."

A few kilometers later the dog raised its leg and pissed all over the American's shoe.

Again the Englishwoman consoled her dog, saying, "Poor itsy-bitsy doggie has a cold in the bladder."

A short while later the dog shat all over the Yank's other shoe. Exasperated, the American stood up, grabbed the dog and threw it out of the window.

At this point the Englishman commented: "You Yanks are a peculiar lot. You speak the wrong language. You live on the wrong side of the ocean. And you, sir, threw the wrong bitch out of the window!"

ohn took his new girl to the movies, which they both enjoyed. After the show he asked what she wanted to do. "I want to get weighed," she said.

He took her to the drugstore, where the machine said her weight was 107 pounds.

Afterwards, she pouted and sulked for the rest of the evening.

When John finally escorted her home, he tried to kiss her at the door, but she pushed him away, saying, "Go on home. I had a wowsy time."

A sweet young thing marries an old man for his money. On their wedding night she jumps into bed and he holds up five fingers.

"Oh, honey," she said with delight, "does that mean five times?"

"No. You can pick one out."

The white missionary had lived in peace in the African village for more than a year but now, as the tribal Chief approached him, he knew there was a problem.

"What is it, Chief?" he asked.

"You in big trouble," the Chief said. "Yesterday white baby was born to my cousin. You only white man in village. We probably decide to roast you alive."

The missionary looked at the hillside behind the Chief. "Look, old man," he said. "I know it looks bad. But you see that flock of white sheep?"

"I see 'em."

"Then notice that black sheep in the flock. It's the only one and there are no other black sheep in the village."

"Okay, okay," said the Chief hastily. "You no tell and I no tell."

A man got into his berth on the train and started to fall asleep when he heard someone in the berth above him say, "Suck, Becky, suck! Blowing is just a figure of speech!"

Three women were boasting about their husbands.

One said, "My Cyrus is Secretary of State," and she proceeded to talk about Cyrus.

The second said, "My Bob is with the agriculture department," and talked about him.

The third said, "My husband Schenley—" and was interrupted by the first woman.

"But isn't Schenley a liquor?"

The third woman said. "You know my husband?"

he attractive wife told her husband she was going on vacation with a girlfriend, but she really went with her long-time wealthy lover, who gave her a beautiful $10,000 mink coat. But she couldn't bring it home so she figured a way. She pawned the mink coat.

She came home and told her husband she had found a pawn ticket, which was really the pawn ticket to her mink coat; and she asked her husband to find out what had been pawned.

Her husband returned and told his wife it was just a cheap watch. The next day his secretary was wearing a $10,000 mink coat.

Every morning, the crowd on Coney Island beach was startled to see a jogger with the build of a pro football player but a head the size of a baseball. Finally, some brave young man got up the nerve to stop him and ask, "What happened to give you such a small head?"

The jogger sadly told the story of finding a magic lamp on the beach, which produced a beautiful genie when rubbed. The genie said, "I now give you one wish. Do you want a quick fuck or a little head?"

The tall blonde model told the clerk: "I don't know the style or color of shoes, but I want low heels." The clerk asked, "To wear with what?" She said, "A short, plump, elderly dress manufacturer."

So this traveling salesman got an audience with the Pope.

"Hey, Father," he said. "Have you heard the joke about the two Polacks who—"

"My son," the Pope said. "I'm Polish."

The salesman thought for a minute. "That's okay, Father," he said. "I'll tell it very slowly."

young girl swallowed a pin when she was eleven and never felt a prick until she turned eighteen.

The on-the-make young executive drinking at the bar was taken aback when the pretty office worker he propositioned snapped at him: "No, buster, you've got the words 'liberated' and 'free' mixed up!"

ittle Johnny was playing airplane with an orange crate.

"Here I am, a real US Army pilot, flying at 30,000 feet," he said to himself and made accompanying flight noises.

Little Mary got interested in what he was doing.

"Can I fly with you, Johnny?" she asked.

"Wait a minute," little Johnny said, as he cut back his engine sounds. "I'll bring her in like a real US Army pilot and then I'll take you up for a spin."

Little Mary climbed on the back of the orange crate.

"Fasten your seat belt," little Johnny commanded. "I'm a real US Army pilot, so prepare for take-off!" He ran through the check list and got airborne at last.

But at 30,000 feet little Mary announced that she had to pee.

"Don't scrub the mission just for that," little Johnny said amiably. "You've got to hang in there for a while yet!"

After a while he noticed a yellow stream between his feet. He glanced around and saw little Mary's snatch exposed.

"Gee that's cute," he said. "Can I touch it?"

She nodded, and he did so very briefly.

"Would you like to kiss it?" she asked.

"I'm not a *real* US Army pilot," little Johnny said.

Define the difference between a snake and a goose.

A snake is an asp in the grass, while a goose is a clasp. . . .

Poem

The Lapper reaps as he sows
With a Ph.D. tongue and a "69" pose.
This twot titillator is much in demand;
He cleans up the kitchen
And thinks that it's grand.

Q: What did Adam say to Eve on the moment that she first came on the scene?
A: You'd better stand back. I don't know how long it's gonna get.

Q: What did the elephant say when he saw the naked man lying on the ground?
A: How can he eat with that thing?

Hey, have you heard about the swell-looking lady sheriff from West Texas?"

"No. What about her?"

"She's got the biggest posse in El Puso."

A young coed, very pretty and sexy, wore an extra tight blouse and skirt which magnified her abundant charms.

She wriggled up to her professor after class and cooed: "Professor, I'd do anything to pass your exam with high marks."

The professor smiled at her, "Anything?"

"Yes, anything. . ."

"Okay," the professor said. "Study!"

A nosy neighbor remonstrated with the woman in the adjourning apartment. "Mrs. Smith, do you think it right that this seventeen-year-old boy spends three hours every night in your apartment?"

Mrs. Smith replied, "It's a platonic friendship. It's play for him and a tonic for me."

CENSORED SHAKESPEARE

I

What's in a name? That which we call a——
By any other name would smell as sweet.

II

You yourself
Are much condemned to have an itching——

III

Thou canst not say I did it; never shake
Thy gory—— at me.

The gynecologist complimented the young woman on his examination table. "Go home and tell your husband to prepare for a baby."

"But I don't have a husband," the girl replied.

"Then, go home and tell your lover."

"But I don't have a lover. I've never had a lover!"

"In that case," the doctor sighed, "go home and tell your mother to prepare for the second coming of Christ."

The well-proportioned black lady was doing her laundry outside on a warm August day in the heart of Alabama. Each time she rubbed downward on the scrubbing board her skirt hiked up over her naked ass.

A jackass looped up behind her and stuck its tongue into her crotch.

Without missing a stroke or even bothering to turn her head, she said: "I don't know who you are, but I does the washin' here every Tuesday and Thursday."

On an isolated part of a beach, a young boy and girl were teasing each other. They were boasting about how one had more than the other of everything.

The nine-year-old boy figured out a way to win the contest. He removed his swim trunks and said, "See, here's something you don't have."

The little girl ran away and returned a few minutes later. She pulled down the bottom of her bathing suit. "My mommy says that with one of these, I can get as many of those as I want."

What did the Polack do with his first fifty-cent piece?
He married her.

A guy walked into the confessional booth and confessed to the priest, "Father, I got laid ten times today!"

The shocked priest exclaimed, "What kind of Catholic are you?"

"I'm not a Catholic at all . . . but I had to tell someone!"

A tour bus traveling through northern Nevada paused briefly at the Mustang Ranch, near Sparks. The guide noted: "We are now passing the largest house of prostitution in America."

A male passenger piped up: "Why?"

Two girls were comparing their experiences at the company's annual Christmas party.

"Did you get laid, Helen?"

"Twice."

"Only twice?"

"Yeah, once by the band and once by the shipping room crew."

She had so many martinis during the party, that when the young virgin was deflowered in the back seat of the Cadillac, her boy friend said shyly, "Well babe, you've lost your olive."

Acomely young blonde was telling he friend at a cocktail party that she was off men for life. "They lie, they cheat, they are just no good. From now on, when I want sex I'll use my vibrator."

"But what if the batteries run out? What will you do?" asked the friend.

"Just what I do with my boy friend—I'll fake an orgasm."

Joanne was eagerly awaiting her blind date's arrival when the doorbell rang and rang. Alice, Joanne's roommate, peeked out the window at the date and let out a great shriek: "My God, you're in it for tonight, Joanne, he's ringing the bell from the bottom of the stairs."

Two girls decided to vacation in Miami Beach together. Neither suspected that the other was also a lesbian. The first night as they shared the same bed for the first time, one rolled over and whispered into her companion's ear, "Let me be frank . . ." at which point the other said soulfully, "No, let me be Frank . . . you can be John."

Alex came home from a business trip to Chicago and found no one home but his daughter Rose, who was crying bitterly.

"What's the matter, darling?" asked Alex.

"Mommy almost died last night," sobbed Rose.

"That's nonsense," said the father. "Why do you say that?"

"Well," said Rose, "you always told us that when we die we'll see God; so when I heard Mommy moaning last night I rushed to her bedroom and she was screaming, 'Oh God, here I come,' and she would have but Uncle Jerry held her down."

D oris had the most beautiful breasts Don had ever seen. His desire to see them fully exposed was his number one passion. Finally he approached Doris and said, "I'll give you $100 if you'll take off your blouse and let me kiss your nipples." Doris, who was always broke, agreed and proceeded to take off her blouse and bra.

Don stared so hard that a wet spot suddenly blossomed on his trousers.

"Well, what are you waiting for?" asked Doris, "don't you have the nerve?"

"I don't have the $100," sighed Don.

Theresa and Jerry shacked up in a barn during a rainstorm. The screwing was so good that they decided to stay the night.

The next morning the farmer heard the commotion in the hayloft and entered his barn shouting, "What's going on in here?"

"We're living on the fruits of love," yelled Jerry.

"Well you better stop soon," said the farmer. "The skins are killing my chickens."

A woman waiting for a train weighed herself on a scale. A card came out with her weight and her fortune: "102 pounds—go over to track two and you'll get fucked."

Astonished but curious, she went over to track two and it actually happened! She was amazed that the scale could predict such a fortune so accurately.

She returned to track one and got on the scale a second time. A card came out with the same weight for her, but this time the fortune read: "Go over to track 12 and you'll fart."

She went over to track 12 and immediately farted several times in a row without any control over her body.

This time she ran back to the scale and got on it a third time. A card popped out with the exact same weight, but the fortune read:

"While you've been fucking and farting around, you missed your damn train!"

One of two gays who were living together suddenly fell in love with the handsome young doctor who had opened up his practice just across the street from their apartment.

"I'd just love to meet him," said one gay to his roommate, "if you have no objections. But I don't know how to go about it."

"I don't mind, sweets. Have your fling. It's easy to meet him. Just pose as one of his patients."

So the first one went to the doctor's office the next day and said his name was Mister Smith.

"What's your problem, Mr. Smith?" the doctor asked.

"Oh, doctor, I have such a terrible pain in my rectum."

"Let's have a look," said the doctor. "Take off your trousers and climb up on the table there."

"Gladly, doctor," lisped the patient eagerly.

The doctor parted his cheeks and looked up inside with a flashlight.

"Holy smoke!" the doctor exclaimed. "No wonder you have pains. Do you realize that you have one dozen American Beauty roses up in there?"

"Never mind the roses," the patient said. "Just read the card!"

A young nun said to her Mother Superior:

"I was out walking in the garden last night and the gardener took me, threw me to the ground and, well, you know . . . Can you give me penance?"

"Go and eat ten lemons," said the Mother Superior.

"But that won't cleanse my sins away."

"I know, but it will wipe that contented grin off your face."

An American, an Englishman, and a Frenchman were discussing a good example of savoir-faire.

"Well," said the American, "if you came home and found your wife in bed with another man and you didn't kill the son of a bitch, that to me is savoir-faire."

"Not quite, chaps," said the Englishman. "If you came home and found your wife in bed with another man and you said, 'Please, sir, carry on,' that's savior-faire."

"Mais non," said the Frenchman. "If you came home and found your wife in bed with another man and you said, 'Please, sir, carry on' and the man was able to continue, *he's* got savoir-faire!"

n a town beside an Indian reservation a beautiful Indian girl was soliciting business, when a prospect asked her rate.

"One hundred dollars!" he exclaimed. "Why, the Indians sold Manhattan for only twenty-four dollars."

"Could be," she smiled and wiggled her hips. "But Manhattan just lies there."

One evening after attending the theater, two gentlemen were walking down the street when they observed a well-dressed, attractive young lady walking just ahead of them. One turned to the other and said, "I'd give fifty bucks to spend the night with that woman." To their surprise, the woman turned and said, "I'll take you up on that." She had a neat appearance and a pleasant voice, so after bidding his friend goodnight the man accompanied the lady to her apartment, where they immediately went to bed.

The following morning the man presented her with twenty-five dollars as he prepared to leave. She demanded the rest of the money, stating, "If you don't give me the other twenty-five I'll sue you for it." He laughed, saying, "I'd like to see you get it on these grounds."

The next day he was surprised when served with a summons ordering his presence in court as defendant. He hurried to his lawyer and explained the details of the case. His lawyer said, "She can't possibly get a judgment against you on such grounds, but it will be interesting to see how her case will be presented."

After the usual preliminaries. the lady's lawyer ad dressed the court as follows:

348

"Your Honor, my client is the owner of a piece of property, a garden spot surrounded by a profuse growth of shrubbery, which property she agreed to rent to the defendant for a specified length of time for the sum of fifty dollars. The defendant took possession of the property, used it extensively for the purpose for which it was rented, but upon evacuating the premises he paid only twenty-five dollars. The rent is not excessive since it was restricted property, and we ask judgment to be granted against the defendant to assure payment of the balance."

The defendant's lawyer was impressed and amused at the way the case had been presented. His defense was therefore somewhat altered from what he had planned. "Your Honor, my client agrees the young lady has a fine piece of property, for a degree of pleasure was derived from the transaction. However, my client found a well on the property, around which he placed his own stones, sunk a shaft and erected a pump, all labor being personally performed by him. We claim these improvements to the property are sufficient to offset the unpaid balance, and that the plaintiff was adequately compensated for the rental of the said property. We therefore ask that the judgment not be granted."

The young lady's lawyer's comeback was this: "Your Honor, my client agrees that the defendant did find a well on the property, and he did make improvements such as described by my opponent; however, had the defendant not known the well existed, he would never have rented the property; also, on evacuating the premises, the defendant moved the stones, pulled out the shaft and took the pump with him. In so doing he not only dragged his equipment through the shrubbery, but left the hole much larger than it was prior to his occupancy, making it easily accessible to little children. We therefore ask judgment be granted."

(She Got It)